Ministering to Intermarried Couples

Charles J. Joanides, Ph.D., LMFT

Ministering to Intermarried Couples:

A Resource for Clergy and Lay Workers

Foreword by
Demetrios Trakatellis
Archbishop of America

GREEK ORTHODOX ARCHDIOCESE OF AMERICA
New York, New York

Published by Greek Orthodox Archdiocese of America
8-10 East 79th Street
New York, New York 10021

ISBN 1-58438-100-0

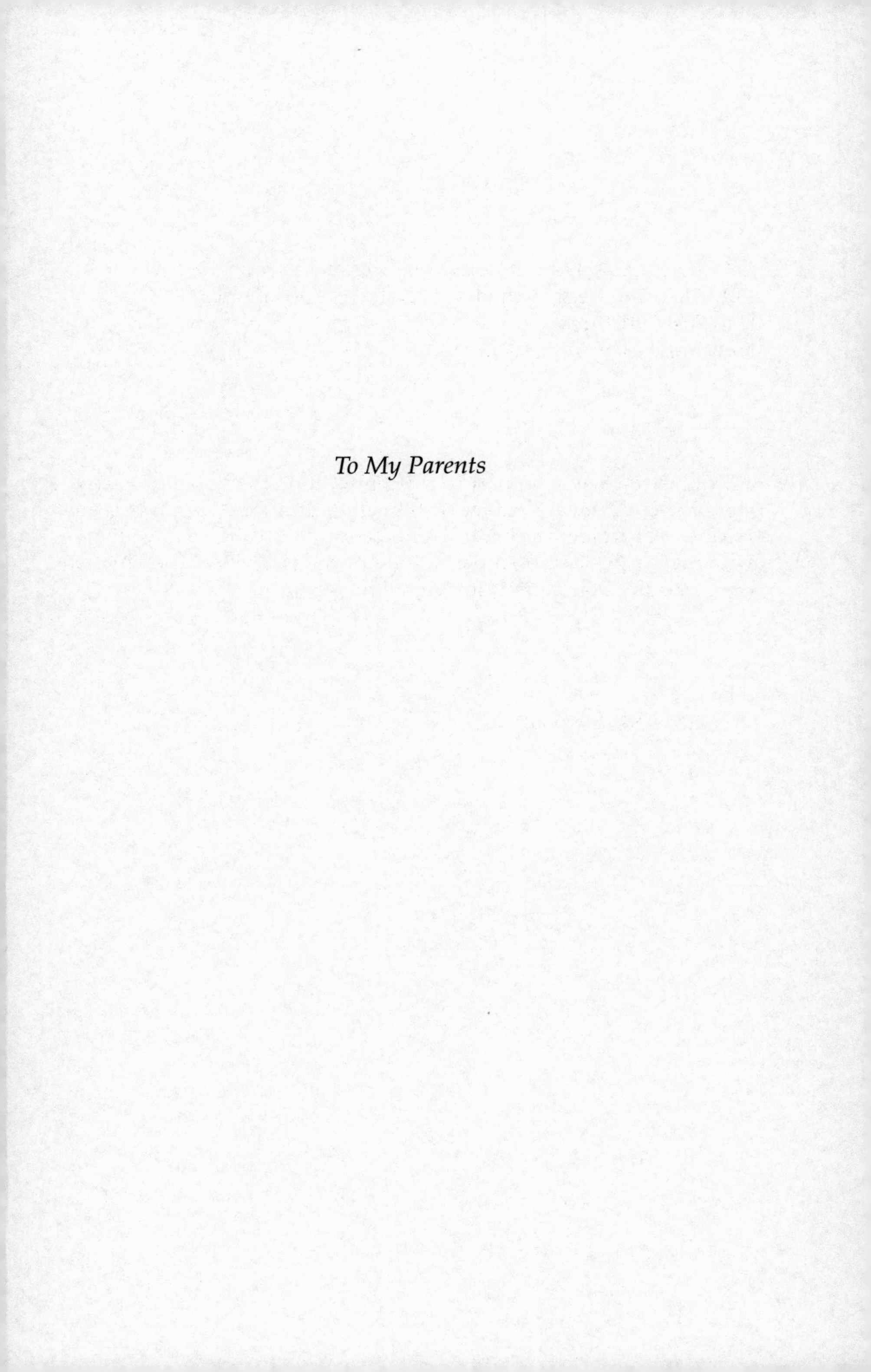

To My Parents

Contents

Foreword *xiii*

Acknowledgments *xvii*

Prologue *xix*

Introduction 1
The Complex Nature of the Intermarriage Challenge 2
Doing More of the Same 4
How to use This Manual 5

Key Reasons Why The Archdiocese Is Concerned 7
Basic Statistics 7
The Importance of Family Among Greek Orthodox Christians 7
Marriage and Family Literature is a Multimillion Dollar Industry 7
Past Clergy and Laity Conferences 8
Summary 8

Local Church's Leadership Role 9
Intermarriage Statistics 9
Couples Want Help 9
A Need for Useful Information 9
Becoming Mindful of Intermarried Couples' Needs 10
Evangelism Facilitated 10
Preventing the Drift Away From our Churches 10
An Overview of a Family Case Study 11
The "X" Family 11
Summary 13

What Is The Intermarriage Research Project (Irp)? 14
Methodology 14
Respondents who Participated 15
Description of Interview Process 16
Techniques to Ensure Trustworthiness 17
Report Style 18

Why Conversion Is not Always an Option 19
Familiarity With One's own Religious Tradition 19
Unfamiliarity With One's Partner's Religious Tradition 20
Doctrinal Differences 20
High Levels of Attachment to One's Cultural Heritage 21
Spouses With Equally low Levels of Religiosity 22
When one of the two Spouses is Nominally Religious 22
When Faith and/or Ethnicity Impacts One's Sense of Self 23
A Renunciation of One's Faith Tradition 23
A Betrayal and Disloyalty of One's Familial Culture 24
A Respect for Extended Family Members' Feelings 24
Growing up in an Inter-Christian Household 25
Minimal Pressure From Family of Origin 25
Conversion is a Personal, Private Issue 26
Imposing Conversion on One's Partner is Against God's Will 26
A Broad, Inclusive View of Their World 27
Dominant American Societal and Cultural Influences 27
Age and Number of Years Married 27
Additional Relevant Factors Related to Non-Orthodox Participants 28
Summary 29

Reasons Why Intermarried Couples Become
Single-church couples 31
Conversion Eliminates Possible Sources of Contention 32
Time, Tolerance, and Education 32
Respectfully Sharing Greek Orthodoxy 32
Weak Religious and Ethnic Connections 33
The Arrival of Children 33
A Love of Orthodoxy 34
Summary 34

HOW INTER-CHRISTIAN COUPLES VIEW THEIR MARRIAGES 36
The Downside of Being Intermarried 38
Inter-Christian but not Inter-Religious 39
Summary 40

A VIEW OF INTERMARRIAGE IN THE GOA 41
A Theory of Intermarriages in the GOA 43
The Developmental Dimension 43
The Social Ecological Dimension 44
Balancing Individual and Couple Needs – Meet Martha and Gus 44
Some Observations 45
Balancing Nuclear Family Needs With Extended Family Needs 47
John and Mary 47
Some Observations 50
Summary 51

CHALLENGES FACING DATING COUPLES 52
General Dating Challenges 52
Typical Individual Challenges 53
Typical Extended Family Challenges 54
Guidelines That Should Assist Clergy and Lay Church Workers 55
An Exercise for the GOYA and YAL 58

CHALLENGES ENGAGED COUPLES ENCOUNTER 61
Typical Extended Family Challenges 62
Pressures to wed in the Greek Orthodox Church 66
Pressure Lessens Before Marriage 68
Guidelines to Assist Clergy and Lay Workers 68

CHALLENGES NEWLYWEDS FACE AFTER MARRIAGE 78
Guidelines That Might Assist Clergy and Lay Leaders 80

FROM CONCEPTION THROUGH YOUNG ADULTHOOD:
CHALLENGES THAT PARENTS ENCOUNTER AS THEIR CHILDREN MATURE 92
Challenges Related to Starting a Family 93
When the Children Begin Maturing 96
When Children Reach Adolescence 100
When Children Begin Leaving Home 105

After the Last Child has Left Home 108
Two Ways to Present This Information to Intermarried Couples 112
Guidelines That Should Assist Clergy and Lay Workers 113
Summary 117

Pastoral Directives 118
Pastoral Directives 119

Pastoral Approaches And Programs 123
What are some basic realities that the Church must consider in its efforts to minister to intermarried couples? 125
How can the Church be more welcoming to the non-Orthodox spouse? 126
How can the Church assist intermarried parents? 128
What are some tangible approaches and programs that can assist intermarried couples? 130
Summary 135

The Value of Premarital Preparation For Intermarried Couples 136
How to use the Materials in this Section 138
Expect Resistance From Some Couples 139
Some Ways to use the Materials 140
A Final Thought 141

Important Premarital Questions that Couples Should Consider 142
Question 1. Have we prayerfully discussed the pros and cons of entering into an inter-Christian marriage versus a single-church marriage? 142
Question 2. Have we prayerfully discussed the pros and cons of becoming an inter-Christian family versus a single-church family? 143
Question 3. Have I been entirely honest with myself about entering an inter-Christian, inter-Church marriage? 145
Question 4. Have I been entirely honest with my spouse about entering an inter-Christian, inter-Church marriage? 146
Question 5. How do I meet my personal religious and spiritual needs in an intermarriage? 147
Question 6. Is it necessary to be acquainted with my spouses' religious tradition? 148
Question 7. Will we worship together or apart? 149
When Both Spouses Have High Religious Commitment 150

Unequal Religious Commitment 151
Spouses with Equally Low Levels of Religiosity 152
Question 8. Have we discussed our religious financial commitments? 153
Question 9. How much of a Greek Orthodox home will we have? 153
Question 10. In which partner's faith tradition will the children be baptized? 154
Question 11. How will the children develop their religious identity? 155
Question 12. How do we deal with our future children's questions regarding our intermarriage? 156
Question 13. How do we honor and respect our own parents in our efforts to raise our children? 158
Question 14. Am I aware of the Orthodox Church's rules pertaining to intermarried couples? 160
Question 15. Do I know why my non-Orthodox in-laws cannot receive the sacraments in the Greek Orthodox Church? 161
Question 16. Have we discussed how we will respect each other's cultural traditions and preferences? 162
Question 17. Is it necessary to be acquainted with my future spouse's ethnic and cultural background? 164

Assessing your Readiness to Intermarry 167

Notes 173

FOREWORD

Analysis of contemporary social trends in the United States reveals a host of complex dynamics which may often seem overwhelming and confusing. Every passing day in our society, people of faith are challenged more and more by the influences of cultural and religious pluralism. These challenges are particularly evidenced by the emergence of a growing social, cultural, and religious phenomenon: *intermarriage*, i.e. marriage between people of differing religions, cultures, or ethnicities. Approached correctly, with faith and love, the pervasiveness of the phenomenon of intermarriage offers to our Greek Orthodox Church in America a tremendous potential for welcoming thousands of others into our communities with the love of Jesus Christ. Efforts to shed light on the origins and operating mechanisms of the dynamics which intermarried couples and their families confront have been especially welcome during the recent decades as our society continues to grow more complex in the context of pluralism and its associated challenges.

Through the work of the Interfaith Research Project (IRP) of the Greek Orthodox Archdiocese of America and the ongoing efforts of Fr. Charles Joanides and other researchers, it has been empirically demonstrated that intermarriage occurs with particularly heightened frequency amongst communities which identify themselves religiously and culturally in ways which stand in a minority relation to mainstream society. This sociological context poses unique challenges to our Greek Orthodox family in the United States, and requires us to better understand our religious identities as Orthodox Christians with an important role to play in shaping the religious landscape of our country and ensuring its vitality for successive generations.

The present, very valuable resource manual for clergy and lay workers, is intended to aid professionals in ministering to the unique needs faced by intermarried couples whose relationship with faith, God, and the Church, intersects with the influences of a religious and cultural pluralistic society. It acknowledges with directness, honesty, love, and the sincere desire to promote spiritual health, the challenges faced by both the Church and intermarried couples as they stand together at the crossroads of this complex and multidimensional intersection. It is offered especially with the hope that our clergy and lay workers may be able to address the crucial pastoral needs of intermarried couples from both an informed psychological and sociological perspective and the perspective of the Orthodox Christian faith, offering true joy and freedom in Christ to the souls of men and women, coming from all walks of life, who are united in the bonds of marriage.

Recalling the essence of St. Paul's explanation concerning marriage and its relation to Christ and the Church (Eph. 5:22-33), we affirm that it is Christ who stands at the center of every marriage, and it is He alone who grants the freedom and ability for all couples to understand their religious and spiritual identities as souls united by the eternal bonds of love. This level of understanding represents the highest and most sophisticated theological and anthropological view of human identity in the perspective of marriage, an identity fully developed with guidance from God. It is an understanding that necessitates patience, commands respect, and calls for toleration on the part of both husband and wife concerning their differences and uniquenesses of person. For intermarried couples, the cultivation of these qualities is especially vital, challenging, and specific, and for this reason it requires the full attention of the

Church, which God unfailingly directs through His infinite love and mercy for humankind.

On behalf of the Greek Orthodox Archdiocese of America, I wish to express my heartfelt thanks to Fr. Charles Joanides for his important work and vital contribution to the growing needs of our faithful and of non-Orthodox spouses throughout our nation, who by God's benevolence today relate to our Holy Orthodox Church in a special way through the bond of marriage. I especially pray that God's ineffable wisdom guides our clergy and lay workers as they minister to intermarried couples and impart to them the saving and healing message of the Gospel of Jesus Christ. May the love of our Lord warm the hearts of all couples currently confronting the challenges of intermarriage, and may the *peace of God that surpasses all understanding* (Phl. 4:7) abide in their souls and their families, as they live more and more under His guidance and blessings.

Archbishop Demetrios
Primate of the Greek Orthodox Church in America

Acknowledgments

Among the numerous individuals who made contributions to this book, the following persons deserve special acknowledgment. His Eminence Archbishop Demetrios should be mentioned first since his pastoral guidance permitted and promoted this work. Support and assistance from His Eminence Metropolitan Iakovos, His Eminence Metropolitan Anthony, His Eminence Metropolitan Maximos, His Eminence Metropolitan Methodios, His Eminence Metropolitan Isaiah, His Grace Bishop Alexios, and His Grace Bishop Nicholas must also be mentioned since their guidance facilitated this work's completion in a timely manner. Rosemary Kromidas Hendrix, M.Ed., CMFT, Dr. Floyd Hendrix, Marilyn Rouvelas and Sub Deacon Nicholas and Nancy Tentzeras deserve special thanks for their many hours of editing and continued encouragement. In alphabetical order, the following individuals who reviewed a working copy of this resource should also be thanked for their many excellent editorial insights: Rev. Fr. Nicholas Anctil, Rev. Fr. Nicholas Apostola, Rev. Fr. Elias Kozar, Rev. Fr. Konstantine Mendrinos, Rev. Fr. James Moskovites, Rev. Dr. Harry Pappas, Presvytera Eleni Paris, Dr. Stephen Muse and Dr. Lewis Patsavos. Gratitude is also extended to Dr. Mick Mayhew for his work as the IRP's research process auditor, and Dr. Philip Mamalakis for his independent analysis of several focus group transcripts. Additionally, and in alphabetical order, Fathers Peter Cade, William Chiganos, Louis Christopulos, Paul Costopoulos, Demetrios Kavadas, Michael Kouremetis, Konstantine Mendrinos, James Paris, Sarantos Serviou, Dennis Strouzas and Elias Velonis should be acknowledged and thanked for agreeing to host focus groups. Fathers

Starvros Akrotirianakis, George Alexson, John Chakos, Athanasios Demos, Steven Denas, Emmanuel Gratsias, Nicholas Harbatis, Dean Hountalas, Basil Kissal, Leo Kopacha, John Kutulas, Nicholas Kyritses, Constantine Makrinos, Paul Palesty, Stylianos Papanikolaou, Nicholas Papedo, Constandinos Pavlakos, John Rallis, Kyriakos Saravelas, George Scoulas, John Tavlarides, Harry Vulopas must also be mentioned for helping to recruit focus group participants. Theo Nicolakis should also be thanked for his many contributions to the Interfaith Marriage Web site. My loving wife Nancy and two children Stephan and Sara also deserve my gratitude for their patience as I labored to complete this work. And finally, while it is impossible to personally mention every intermarried spouse who contributed to the thick, rich descriptions and observations contained in this resource, a special mention is offered to the 376 respondents who willingly participated in one of the focus groups, and, or reviewed the information on the Interfaith Marriage Web site www.interfaith.goarch.org and provided feedback.

I wish to express my thanks to Faye and Wayne Sturdivant for the use of their wedding photograph on the cover.

In XC,
Rev. Fr. Charles Joanides, Ph.D., LMFT

Prologue

Father Charles,

It's hard for me not to think of you every time I hear the word separation, or when Nicole and I celebrate our marital reunion. Timing can be a funny thing sometimes. It was a year ago today when I asked Nicole to remarry me in front of the kids.... In a recent autobiography that my youngest daughter wrote in school, she mentioned that the happiest day of her life was that day when mommy and daddy got back together.

May God continue to bless you, your family and ministry.

Joe

I received this e-mail the other day. God knows it came at a good time. It lifted my spirits and confirmed a message that lies deep within my heart and soul – the best things in life really are free.

A few years ago, Joe and his wife came to me. They were having some serious marital problems. With one foot out the door, both argued their cases convincingly and with great passion. "She's self-centered... He works too hard and never has time for us... She's into some New Age religion... He's been unfaithful... I think she's been unfaithful... He doesn't understand... She's ungrateful...." Quite frankly, the flow and regularity of these types of comments seemed endless.

We went around in circles for three sessions. Little was accomplished. It was exhausting for all of us. In the midst of this crucible, during the third session, I was reminded of something a valued mentor had once shared. She said, "If you're working harder than they are, you're out gunned and over matched. There's no way therapy will succeed."

At that moment, I stopped the session, and offered the following observations with no apology. "Listen, I'm willing to go the distance with you to save your marriage, but you both have to feel the same way. Until you're invested in change, I can't do any more."

Both partners seemed stunned. They didn't know what to say.

When you work with couples, there are certain moments that I sometimes refer to as, "aha" moments. They are very ephemeral in nature, and they can quickly disappear if you're not tracking the process carefully. Fortunately, I was plugged in enough to discern this opportunity. "Let's stop for now," I continued in a respectful manner. "I can't do anymore. We're simply wasting our time and your money. Call me if you want to continue." They knew I was right. The session ended with no objections.

I didn't hear anything from this couple for several months. I figured they either slipped back into their old unhealthy habits, stopped trying and decided to get a divorce or found another therapist. Then one day, without warning, Joe contacted me. He explained that he wanted to continue therapy, but his wife didn't. He said "she's not ready. But I've been thinking about what you said. You were right. With God's help, I'm determined to do all I can to save my marriage and family."

I invited him to come back. We started individual marital therapy that would eventually lead us to some couple's work. Today this couple and family is back together - happier and more hopeful than ever.

Unless spouse abuse or some other form of abuse is taking place, I've come to believe that a substantial number of marriages that end in divorce can be saved. Admittedly, it takes time and commitment, but it's possible. I've seen it happen.

The effects of divorce are acutely severe. Perhaps that's why divorce is referenced as one of the top psychosocial stressors in the *Diagnostic and Statistical Manual of Mental Disorders IV*. Divorce correlates with adult depression, poverty, children's poor school performance, children's low self-esteem, adolescent crime and violence, out of wedlock birth rates and child abuse – and this is only a partial list.

Even though this book was written to facilitate the work that clergy and lay workers do with intermarried couples and their families, it was also written to encourage us all to consider what we are doing for all the marriages and families in the communities we serve. Information from the Interfaith Marriage Research Project (IRP) indicates that our faithful are looking to the church to provide them with help in these areas of their lives. Due in large part to the conflicting messages that society sends them, many are confused and want the church to take a more proactive role in helping them with the marital and family challenges they are facing.

I don't know why the Church's voice has failed to resonate with regard to many of the important issues that face its members' marriages and families today – but it has. My prayer is that this book will make a small contribution toward ameliorating the unhealthy climate that marriages and families find themselves in today.

Somehow the human sciences have either snatched this responsibility from the Church's hands, or we've relinquished it. But thankfully, things are changing. Society has realized that the social sciences don't have all the answers.

Please don't misunderstand me. I'm one of those individuals who believes that a cross fertilization between human science and religion can prove beneficial to the Church's faithful. As we struggle to protect the integrity of what we believe in a post-Christian society, human science can inform our work in many positive ways, so long as we remember to defer to Divine revelation when the two conflict.

God is reaching out to marriages and families throughout our great nation in a positive way. A movement to decrease the divorce rates and promote marriage and family life is under way at all levels of our nation, even as I write. And many people of faith are leading this effort. I believe that our heavenly Father is calling us to become a part of this holy effort. We shouldn't be left standing on the sidelines. One way to start is by creating a ministry for the intermarried couples and families in your parishes, and then seeking to expand it to all marriages and families.

Rev. Fr. Charles Joanides, Ph.D., LMFT
March 13, 2002

Introduction

We live in a secular, postmodern age[1]. The ideas that impact the public and private spheres of our lives are decidedly post-Christian and postmodern. As such, it is not uncommon for members of our society to view marriage as a human construction that has evolved through social consensus. It is also not unusual to hear people conceptualizing marriage as a private, personal decision that serves to enhance emotional, social, economic, and psychological well-being. Similarly, it is also not odd for people to consider marriage disposable when it ceases meeting their needs[2].

The Orthodox Church does not find these perceptions of meaningful significance in its own efforts to conceptualize marriage. From an Orthodox perspective, marriage is lifted out of a pragmatic, mundane, legal and secular context. It is recontextualized within a life in the Father, Son, and Holy Spirit. Marriage from a Christian and Orthodox perspective is not predicated on what is deemed socially, politically, legally, economically, and, or philosophically correct. The Orthodox view is entirely dependent on certain divinely revealed truths that have emerged as God has manifested His truth to people. Among these divine truths, the following observations are central to the Orthodox Church's conception of marriage:

- Marriage is fundamentally dependent upon God's revealed truth, as manifested in our Church's Sacramental, Christological, and Trinitarian theology.
- The meaning of marriage from an Orthodox perspective seeks to meet humankind's spiritual needs, as well as our physical, emotional, economic, and social needs.

• Marriage is understood as a God-given way of existence, and a precious eternal gift from God that must be cherished. To quote St. John Chrysostom, "From the beginning God in His providence has planned this union of man and woman.... There is no relationship between human beings so close as that of husband and wife."[3] It is not simply a human construction that has evolved through social consensus, but is most completely understood as man and woman enter into holy matrimony in prayerful synergy with God through the Father, Son and Holy Spirit.

• An Orthodox perspective of marriage is not based on secular, legalistic concepts such as justice and egalitarianism. Orthodox marriages are firmly founded on Christ-like, self-sacrificial agape, forgiveness, and mercy. The wisdom contained in the following verses impact marital interactions and transactions and are illustrative of this latter observation. "...whoever would be great among you must be your servant, and whoever would be first among you must be your slave; even as the Son of man came not to be served but to serve, and to give his life as a ransom for many" (Mt. 20: 26 – 27).

• Marriage functions to draw persons into God's Kingdom. It exhorts them to live Christ-like existences in a community of persons (otherwise called the Community of Marriage), and allows them to become co-eternal participants in the process of divine life and perfection.

• As understood by Orthodox Holy Tradition, marriage assists individuals in their efforts to become more complete persons and realize their full humanness.

• Marriage calls a man and woman toward a God-given "oneness" that only they will share. This God-given oneness is multidimensional. Every component of their bio-psycho-social humanness is called to participate in this oneness[4].

The Complex Nature of the Intermarriage[5] Challenge

In light of these presuppositions, the first and most important point is that the intermarriage challenge is a complex issue. Additionally, there are numerous complex pastoral and theological questions and concerns that have been raised and given careful attention. Here is a sampling of some of these questions.

• Should we be developing pastoral approaches to address the intermarriage challenge in our Archdiocese?

• Are such initiatives simply an indication of the Church's compliance to social pressure?

• From an Archdiocesan level, can we develop pastoral approaches toward intermarriages that will not violate and, or dilute our Orthodox understanding of marriage?

Those who espouse these and other similar concerns and questions wonder how two people from different faith and cultural traditions (and in some instances, racial backgrounds) can achieve the religious, spiritual, physical, psychological, and social "oneness" to which our Lord has called married couples. Such thinkers also argue that the church should not be in the business of enabling these types of misguided decisions, but should vigilantly seek to protect the church's beliefs from being diluted by the secular, postmodern society in which it is embedded.

While this position is very compelling indeed, statistics indicate that nearly two out of every three (63%) marriages conducted in the Greek Orthodox Archdiocese of America (GOA) during the last 20 years are inter-Christian[6]. Other similar data suggest that during the 1990s some dioceses performed more Orthodox/Catholic marriages than Orthodox/Orthodox marriages[7]. Moreover, there is no evidence to suggest that these statistical trends will reverse themselves in the future[8].

In the face of such overwhelming figures, the Orthodox Church (at all levels) has engaged in considerable dialogue, and questions such as the following have been discussed and debated[9].

• Should we begin labeling these types of marriages as "deviant?"

• Should the Church address these trends by assuming a condemnatory posture toward those who intermarry?

• If we choose to disapprove, or stigmatize these marriages, what are the consequences of taking such an approach?

• Can the Church continue to disregard the overwhelming numbers of intermarriages being conducted across our Archdiocese?

• Should the Church embrace the intermarriage trends proactively, and consider how and if *"economia"* can be employed?

• Should the Church begin carefully addressing this issue in an effort to seek effectual ways of ministering to this growing segment of its faithful?

As a result of a substantial amount of prayerful conversation that has taken place prior to the development of this manual, it should be stated that the Church has determined that ignoring these trends and labeling them problematic and, or deviant, is not a solution. On the contrary, the Church has resolved to examine this issue carefully in an effort to fulfill part of its divine calling — to "...make disciples of all nations, baptizing them in the name of the Father, Son and Holy Spirit, teaching them to observe all that I have commanded you" (Mt. 28: 19-20). Moreover, the information contained in this manual demonstrates its resolve (at the level of the GOA) to begin reaching out more effectively to this growing group of faithful.

Doing more of the same

One of the greatest mistakes people make when seeking to resolve a problem is to utilize "more of the same" failed types of solutions. In other words, they look for solutions by employing more of the same types of strategies. However, many important solutions to problems have resulted when individuals have thought about a given problem in a slightly different way, and implemented solutions that were qualitatively different.

For example, with regards to marriage, in the latter part of his life and ministry, St. John Chrysostom determined that the Church's theological perspective regarding marriage had gone askew as a result of certain neoplatonic influences that had infiltrated the manner in which it viewed marriage. Moreover, only after a series of sermons when St. John thinks of marriage outside of the limited perspective from which it was being conceptualized, does a broader and more holistic Orthodox view of marriage begin to emerge.[10]

In a similar manner, this manual is designed to encourage qualitatively different thinking with regards to the intermarriage challenge facing the GOA. Furthermore, in an effort to accomplish this objective, the information in this manual will seek to answer the following questions:

- Why is the Archdiocese concerned with intermarriages?
- On a local level, why should we be concerned with intermarriages?
- What unique challenges do intermarried couples experience over the marital life cycle?
- What are some of the salient social ecological challenges that intermarried couples face?
- What are some examples of programs and approaches that can be utilized to minister more effectively to intermarried couples?
- What are some suggestions and guidelines that can help clergy during the premarital preparation process with perspective inter-Christian and intercultural couples?

How to use this Manual

This resource was developed to be used in tandem with a recently published book entitled, *When You Intermarry,*[11] a resource developed for intermarried couples and their families. When utilized together, these resources should be of great assistance to clergy and lay leaders.

I suggest that it be read in digestible portions, and kept on reserve for future reference. Because the nature of this challenge is complex and multidimensional, I anticipate that you will find the table of contents useful after your initial reading.

Whichever way you choose to use this manual, I pray that you as clergy and lay workers[12] will find its contents helpful in your efforts to minister to the intermarried couples and their families in your churches and dioceses. I also anticipate that the information that follows will stimulate others to build upon this work and create fresh, new pastoral approaches that will serve to assist the church in its efforts to embrace this challenge.

Chapter One

KEY REASONS WHY THE ARCHDIOCESE IS CONCERNED

Basic Statistics

From 1949 –1989 inter-Christian marriages increased nine-fold in the Greek Orthodox Archdiocese of North and South America. In 1949 there were approximately 400 inter-Christian marriages conducted and by 1989 there were about 3600 performed.[13] Additionally, about 63% of all marriages performed in the Archdiocese between 1976 – 98 were inter-Christian.[14] This means that nearly two-thirds of our young people married a non-Orthodox Christian from the late 1970s through the 1990s. If we were to include the marriages that are not conducted in our churches, some estimates suggest that the figure of intermarriages is closer to 80%.[15]

The Importance of Family Among Greek Orthodox Christians

Both Greek studies scholars[16] and our theologians[17] agree that families are of fundamental importance to Greek Orthodox Americans. Family scholars[18] also argue that individual well-being is predicated on family well-being. Family scholars also maintain that healthy marriages contribute to individual and family well-being and vice versa. They maintain that physical, emotional and financial well-being is positively correlated with marital satisfaction.[19]

Marriage and Family Literature is a Multimillion Dollar Industry

We live in a market place of ideas. There are numerous "experts" seeking to compete with the church in an effort to market their ideas to our marriages and families. It is incumbent upon our church to start addressing some of these issues, otherwise someone else will. What the consequences of this will be is anyone's guess. However, one observation seems rather clear and may provide us with some clues. Research suggests that our society has had a decided impact on how young adults view marriage. Research also indicates that fewer adults are willing to commit themselves to a long-term marriage relationship as a result of the difficulties their parents experienced and the high divorce rates.[20]

Past Clergy and Laity Conferences

As early as 1974, Clergy and Laity Congresses have identified interfaith marriages as a challenge (not a threat) that should be examined more carefully.[21]

The report given in 1996 from the Committee on Interchurch and Interfaith Marriages[22] began with the following statement:

"Interfaith marriages and interchurch households are the reality. To ignore that reality, to maintain a rigidity of outlook in regards to these couples and families would mean that in practice, we would be closing our doors to the very children, adults and families who are the church's future."

Summary

Why is the Archdiocese concerned with intermarriages?

- Two out of every three marriages performed in our communities are inter-Christian.
- Families are of central importance to Greek American's well-being.
- Healthy marriages lead to healthy families.
- Social scientists are writing about marriages and families from numerous philosophical perspectives and our Orthodox voice must also be heard.
- For decades, Clergy-Laity Congresses have maintained that intermarried couples in our Archdiocese, Dioceses and local churches, have special needs that must be identified, respected and addressed in a timely manner. Otherwise, many Orthodox Christians will drift away from the Orthodox Church.

Chapter Two

LOCAL CHURCH'S LEADERSHIP ROLE

Just as the Archdiocese and our Dioceses are concerned with the intermarriage challenge, local parish leadership must also be concerned for the following reasons:

Intermarriage Statistics

A substantial number (63%) of the marriages conducted in our local churches are inter-Christian in composition, with many parishes reporting figures as high as 90 – 95%. Ignoring the needs of these marriages will likely have a negative impact on many local churches. Logically, local churches which offer quality attention to this growing group of faithful will prosper, while communities that choose to ignore them will likely suffer some negative consequences in membership and revenue.

Couples Want Help

Results from the Intermarriage Research Project[23] (IRP) suggest that intermarried spouses and couples are clamoring for some direction and support in their efforts to cultivate functional, healthy and faith-centered marriages and families. They are increasingly looking to their local churches for assistance in this effort. Churches showing sensitivity for their needs are more likely to be successful in retaining intermarried couples' commitment and participation.

A Need for Useful Information

Americans appreciate information in order to make decisions concerning the issues and challenges they face. They do not like authority figures arbitrarily telling them what to do.[24] They would rather have the information in their possession in order to make well informed decisions. Keeping this in mind, unless we are able to offer information along with respectful direction to our couples and families, our faithful are likely to turn elsewhere for answers in an effort to address their marital and family challenges.[25]

Becoming Mindful of Intermarried Couples' Needs

Just as we are sensitive to the needs of our children, adolescents, young adults, single-church couples and families and our elderly, we must strive to become increasingly more aware of the unique needs of this growing segment of our church's faithful. As the contents of this resource will show, these couples have special needs due in part to their religious and cultural differences. When clergy and lay leaders become mindful of these needs, this will have a more positive impact on the quality of ministry that is offered to intermarried couples and their families.

Evangelism Facilitated

In our efforts to become more sensitive and attentive to the intermarried couples and families who attend the GOA, we will become more aware of how the needs of our congregations are changing as a result of the new faces in our parishes. Making adjustments to accommodate the needs of intermarried couples should thus assist the local church in its efforts to become more inclusive, and by extension, more evangelical in its approach to ministry.

Preventing the Drift Away from Our Churches

Finally, striving to develop a vision of ministry that makes all people feel comfortable in our churches is a God given objective that is unequivocally God's will, and inherently part and parcel of our Holy Greek Orthodox Tradition. However, results from the IRP indicate that many local churches are not doing enough for intermarried couples and their families. As it will become clearer in successive chapters, many members of these marriages and families appear to be slowly drifting away from the Orthodox Church. As such, something must be done to reverse this process. If this present trend continues, it is likely that large numbers of our children and grandchildren will lose touch with their Greek Orthodox background.

An Overview of a Family Case Study

I want to end this chapter by offering a few statistics from a family case study I recently completed. This work examined certain trends as they relate to religious affiliation over the course of four generations in one family. To protect their identity, I will call this family, the "X" family. While this information cannot be generalized to the greater population of Greek American families, other research examining these trends suggests that the trends and statistics I will share may be more pervasive than any of us would care to admit.[26] Further research is necessary to examine these trends more closely.

The "X" Family

In 1918, Grigorios and Vasiliki would immigrate to this country from one of the Greek islands. They would reside in a Greek neighborhood in one of the large cities in the Northeast. Grigorios would sell newspapers, shine shoes and peddle fruit. Eventually he would obtain work in a large factory. While they each envisioned staying in America for only a few years, they would never see Greece again.

They would be blessed with five children, three boys and two girls. These five children would be part of the World War II generation. After the war, all five would marry and eventually move into the suburbs and live a middle-class existence. Four of the five siblings (80%) would marry Greek Americans. These five couples would have 14 offspring who would be considered part of the Baby Boomer generation.

All 14 Baby Boomers would be baptized in the Greek Orthodox Church. Most would live middle-class existences, while a few would obtain advanced degrees and live upper-middle-class existences. Of these 14 children, 10 would intermarry (71%), one would marry another Greek American, one would remain single and two would cohabitate but never marry. Of the 10 who would intermarry, 5 would choose to marry outside of the Orthodox Church. These five, together with the two cohabiting individuals, do not attend the Greek Orthodox Church (50%). The other five who would intermarry in the Orthodox Church continue to retain some connections to the church, as does the individual who would marry a Greek Orthodox Christian and the individual who never married (50%). In addition, this generation would be blessed with 28 children – two of the 28 would be born out of wedlock. These children would be part of the "X" generation. Of these offspring, 16 (57%) would either not be baptized or be baptized in a non-Orthodox Church.

While these trends and statistics are not typical of every family who has had some affiliation with the GOA over the last four generations, after investigating this issue for the past five years, I would maintain that they are typical of many of the families whom we only see on Easter, Christmas and during a family event. I would also argue that these trends are suggestive of some of the salient challenges that face everyone who serves the GOA. As Archdiocesan statistics, other research, this case study, and information from the IRP indicate, it appears that each successive generation's connections to the GOA have attenuated. I am thus compelled to ask the following questions: Why is this happening? What can be done to stop and reverse these trends? What should the church be doing differently?

I think that many people who care about the future well-being of the GOA are also concerned about this topic. Perhaps that is the reason why the workshops dealing with the intermarriage issue were packed in Orlando and Philadelphia at the last two Clergy Laity Congresses. And while most do not have a sophisticated understanding of this challenge, they know that this is a burning issue that must be addressed. The remainder of this resource will strive towards answering these and other similar questions. However, it must be stressed here that all of the questions and answers are not contained in this book, and much more attention must still be given to other related topics such as interreligious marriages. Nevertheless, it is my belief that this information provides a good starting point for further work in this area in your local parish and at other levels in the GOA. My prayer is that it will serve some of your needs.

Summary

Why should local church leadership be concerned with the intermarriage challenge?

• Spouses and couples are asking for assistance and support in their efforts to cultivate healthy, functional marriages and families.

• Intermarried couples are asking for useful information to help them address their many challenges.

• Becoming more sensitive and being attentive to the unique needs that intermarried couples and their families encounter can have a positive affect on every local church's future.

• Increased focus on this population can help churches become more evangelical minded at the local level.

• Results from the IRP indicate that intermarried couples and their families are slowly drifting away from the GOA. An increased outreach at the local level can help stop this drift.

Chapter Three

What is the Interfaith Research Project (IRP)?

Together with previous work done in this area, the Interfaith Research Project's (IRP) initial and primary objective was to document the lived experiences and challenges of inter-Christian couples[27] who worship in our churches. This documentation served to amplify a key voice absent in previous writing concerned with the intermarriage challenge in the GOA.[28] In designing this study, I selected an approach that would enhance the Church's efforts to reach out to this growing group of faithful.

Methodology

Focus groups are widely used by successful corporations to determine marketing needs. Not only do they ascertain what consumers need and want, but also help to meet these needs.[29] Focus groups were utilized in much the same manner in this study. The difference is that the methodology was tailored to account for the idiosyncratic religious and spiritual nature of this study.

Rather than marketing a product, the purpose of this research was to seek to facilitate religious and spiritual development. With this goal in mind, I sought to utilize focus groups for the following purposes:

(a) Focus groups were used as a means to enter into the minds and hearts of intermarried spouses and couples to discover their lived experiences about religion and Greek Orthodoxy, and to assist the Church in its efforts to address their unique challenges.

(b) The information generated from these focus groups would facilitate the development of resource materials, programs, and policies that would assist pastors and lay leaders in their efforts to minister to this growing group of faithful.

(c) The IRP was conducted to help the church in its efforts to facilitate inter-Christian couples' and families' religious and spiritual development: to God's glory and our salvation.

Respondents Who Participated

After receiving each Diocesan Hierarch's blessings, priests were contacted in each diocese in an initial effort to recruit couples for this study. In total, 38 priests offered valuable assistance by identifying potential informant couples for the IRP.

Once priests in each diocese submitted couples' names, and a pool of potential couples was assembled, couples were recruited by phone. During the selection process, I was particularly interested in including couples who could articulate their experience. Groups of participants who have as much in common as possible were formed. This technique made it less likely that participants would be debating each other, and more likely that a recursive, reciprocal dialogic process would unfold. This would allow participants to build upon each other's observations and descriptions.

I also sought to include as many different perspectives as possible. Spouses and individuals with high, moderate and low levels of religious and, or ethnic attachments were thus recruited. Converts, immigrants, first, second, third, fourth and fifth generation participants were represented. Participants from mixed ethnic and religious backgrounds were also included. Baby Boomers and Generation "X" couples were also recruited. This was done to ensure that the contents of this study would reflect a wide range of voices and perspectives that belong to the population of faithful in this particular investigation.

A total of 202 participants responded as couples in one of 20 focus groups that were conducted from April 1998 – December 1999. Each couple was inter-Christian and in most cases intercultural. Some were further identified as inter-Christian, intercultural, and interracial. Respondents were from 27 different cities, with some level of affiliation with one of 21 different Greek Orthodox communities.

Two different types of focus groups were conducted in each diocese. One type of focus group was comprised of couples that were part of the "X" Generation (20-34), and a second type of focus group was comprised of Baby Boomers (35-50). This decision was made in an effort to isolate any idiosyncratic differences and needs that might exist from one generation to the next.

In addition to focus group participants, 174 individuals who reviewed the results posted on the Interfaith Marriage Web site took part in this process.[30] These individuals examined the results that were periodically posted and offered observations and descriptions on feedback forms. The inclusion of these individuals served to reinforce the credibility of the information that was emerging and infuse additional richness into the research's developing descriptions and theoretical conceptualizations.

When focus group participants involved in the IRP are considered along with those individuals who visited the Interfaith Marriage Web site, results from the IRP reflect over 376 intermarried spouses' descriptions and observations. This is an exceptionally large number of respondents for a qualitative study, when one considers that most qualitative studies of this type generally involve a substantially smaller number of participants.[31]

Description of Interview Process

Before each focus group was conducted, individual participants were asked to complete a 24 item questionnaire[32] that was designed to (a) gather demographic information, (b) identify factors contributing to their decision to intermarry, and (c) gather attitudinal information about intermarriage.

In addition, prior to conducting each focus group, couples were reminded that they were not simply sharing information with the moderator/researcher, but would indirectly be speaking to the Archbishop, Metropolitans, Bishops, Priests, and lay leaders of the GOA. I also sought to cultivate respect and candor for all perspectives. Confidentiality was assured to each respondent.

Open-ended questions were utilized to generate conversation.[33] Examples of the type of questions utilized follow: What has it been like being intermarried? What have been some of your surprises, blessings, challenges, and difficulties?

Open-ended questions also tended to change as the research process unfolded. When I determined that a point of saturation was reached (a point when essentially redundant information was emerging) new questions were constructed and new areas of inquiry were probed and introduced into the research process. This approach ensured that a broad, systematic description of intermarried spouses' and couples' personal experiences would emerge.

Techniques to Ensure Trustworthiness

In an effort to generate theory and description, a grounded theory approach,[34] together with a naturalistic inquiry approach[35] were utilized. Moreover, each of these approaches sought to address reliability and validity issues so as to ensure the trustworthiness of a given research project. By following numerous techniques and approaches that both of these research protocols describe, I sought to strengthen the reliability and validity of this study. Examples of techniques utilized to ensure that the results from this study were not reflective of my personal biases, but representative of participants' views, are briefly described below.

Twenty member checks were conducted regularly after each focus group. Member checks are essentially follow-up interviews that were employed after the analysis of each focus group. Member checks were conducted by telephone with members of each focus group. These interviews lasted about 60 – 90 minutes, and allowed me to share the analysis with one – three members from selected groups. This technique helped ensure that my analysis did not conflict with participants' perceptions, thus preventing the research process from being contaminated by my own biases.

A doctoral student familiar with the methodology and analysis procedures was also recruited to provide an independent analysis of a few select transcripts. My results were then crosschecked with this independent analysis as an additional technique to safeguard against researcher bias.

Theoretical and coding notes resembling a diary were also kept on each focus group. In addition to the researcher's analysis of each group, these notes functioned to stimulate my growing understanding of the culture I was investigating. They also served to guide my methodological decisions, and assisted the process auditor in his efforts to provide a process audit of this research. This technique also ensured that the research process was being guided by the information that was emerging.

A process auditor who was not directly involved in this research, but is intimately familiar with this type of research, was also enlisted to review the research and to determine if the conclusions were supported by the evidence that emerged during the research process. This technique further ensured that the information that emerged was both reliable and valid.

Report Style

Rather then providing the reader with numerous statistical charts and tables that concern themselves with a discreet set of variables, the nature of this research was essentially qualitative. As such, the findings from the IRP will essentially resemble a story. Unlike most stories that are told from the perspective of one individual however, the story that follows has emerged systematically, and is reflective of the observations and descriptions of over 376 intermarried spouses who have some degree of affiliation with a Greek Orthodox Church. Furthermore, this story will be broken in numerous parts, to make it easier for you to follow, and more importantly, to use this manual. You can also expect to encounter some figures. These figures have been constructed as a way to visually depict some of the key components of this story, and have been employed in an effort to chronicle this story in an efficient and discernible manner.

Chapter Four

Why Conversion Is not Always an Option[36]

People have opinions about every issue under the sun. This is especially true if someone is speaking from personal experience about a given issue. It is at these times when it seems that people speak with the most self-assurance and conviction. An excerpt from an e-mail that was sent to the Archdiocese illustrates this point. In this e-mail the writer offers some simple advice to those considering an inter-Christian marriage.

"We lost three-plus years in marriage skirting the issue of religion. A minister frequented our home to give advice.... He plainly said, 'Pick one.' We did, and life instantly became simpler and more meaningful. My advice to those considering an inter-Christian marriage is to pick one partner's church and become a one-church, one-faith family."

While this "just do it" approach concerning conversion may have helped this couple, results from the IRP indicate that this one-size-fits-all advice is not suitable in every situation. Just as there are numerous good reasons that compel couples to become single-faith couples and families, there are also a number of good reasons why couples choose to remain intermarried and do not consider conversion an appropriate choice. This chapter will present a number of important reasons that influence couples to enter and remain in an inter-Christian marriage. And even though all these reasons may not necessarily relate to every inter-Christian couple that worships in the GOA, one or more will apply.

Familiarity With One's own Religious Tradition

Many participants repeatedly indicated that they could not imagine themselves belonging to a faith tradition other than their own. When pressed to elaborate, many described a familiarity, affection, and comfort with their religious tradition that was integrally important in their efforts to worship God. One participant stated, "I enjoy singing certain Protestant hymns. They allow me to get into the right spirit." In another focus group a Catholic participant stated, "I like going to the Catholic Church because I know what's going on. I get to participate more with the priest, instead of just standing there and listening to someone else." In another group, a Greek Orthodox participant stated, "One reason I could never consider conversion is because I'm familiar with my religion. When I'm in church and I smell the incense, see the icons, hear the priest and choir, I feel close to God. So, conversion wasn't a real option for me."

Unfamiliarity With One's Partner's Religious Tradition

Participants also stated that their lack of familiarity with their partner's religious tradition tended to stifle their efforts to worship at the same intimate level. "I tried going to my spouse's church," stated one Greek Orthodox participant, "but it just didn't do anything for me. I guess I need to hear the chanting, see the icons, and smell the incense." The following remarks by a Roman Catholic participant were also typical of how many non-Orthodox felt about their Greek Orthodox partner's faith tradition. "When I go to the Catholic Church, I know the Mass by heart and what's going to happen next. It's not like that when I attend the Greek Church."

Numerous participants in this study tended to view conversion as a risky option that might function to compromise or impair their religious and spiritual development, as well as their relationship with God. "I guess I'm happy where I am," stated one respondent. "If I decided to change, I just don't know how that might affect my relationship with God."

Doctrinal Differences

Participants' discomfort with some of the doctrinal differences that existed between their religious traditions were also occasionally alluded to as factors that inhibited them from considering conversion. "I just don't understand all the fasting rules. But not only that, sometimes it seems as if everyone's got their own take on the rules. I mean some Greeks fast one way, and others fast another way... it's very confusing and frustrating for me." Conversely, in other instances some Greek Orthodox participants stated that their non-Orthodox partner's faith tradition sometimes had ambiguous rules and guidelines. "At least I kind of know where my Church stands on certain moral and church issues, even though I may not always agree. Some church's positions on issues like abortion and women priests, for example, are too hard, or too fuzzy, and that bothers me."

High Levels of Attachment to One's Cultural Heritage

Since Greek Orthodoxy was often conceptualized in ethnoreligious terms, several non-Greek Orthodox with strong ethnic attachments stated that their moderate to strong ethnic ties prevented them from considering conversion. For example, one respondent said the following: "Thinking about converting is a very emotional subject for me. Whenever I consider this idea, I think about my ethnic background and know that I could not convert because you almost have to become a little Greek to belong to this Church, and that would mean I would have to become a little less Brazilian."

Greek Orthodox participants also repeatedly stated that their strong attachments to their ethnic background precluded any serious discussions about conversion to their spouse's faith tradition. These participants associated conversion with a loss of an intrinsically important part of themselves. The following comment is indicative of numerous similar comments, "If I were to leave the Church, I would feel like I was leaving something important about who I am and what makes me tick.... A large part of why I go to the Greek Church is because I am Greek, and my Greek heritage means something to me."

Spouses with Equally low Levels of Religiosity

Observations from spouses with an equally low level of religious and cultural commitment were qualitatively different from those with a moderate to high level of commitment. When religion did not assume a prominent role in their lives, this factor inhibited a couple from considering conversion. Results from the IRP suggest that spouses with low levels of religious commitment have very little incentive to become single-faith couples because religion has a peripheral impact on their lives. These respondents frequently stated that changes in their religious status did not seem "cost effective," since conversion requires "time" and "effort" and "a commitment to a way of living and thinking that may not always fit with our current world view."

When one of the two Spouses is Nominally Religious

Nominally religious participants often admitted that because religion did not play an important role in their lives, their mate's religious affiliation was not a chief consideration during the dating process, nor was their mate's religious affiliation perceived as playing a primary role in their marriage's well-being. Other factors such as their spouse's personality, family values, worldview, and their mutual love for one another were mentioned as being more important reasons to explain why these types of participants were attracted to their mate, decided to marry their spouse, and why they remained married. One nominally religious spouse's remarks are reflective of these latter observations. He stated, "Even though she's Catholic, when we were dating I looked at the person, her values, her family… and not the religion. Since I'm not real religious, that's what made me feel strongly about marrying her. So I suppose conversion was not, and will continue to be a non-issue for me personally."

These types of respondents also observed that they had not considered conversion because they could not perceive how conversion might improve the quality of their lives. Their observations suggested that their religious and cultural differences were only occasional irritants in their lives that did not justify the effort it might take to convert. "Once in a while religion comes up as a problem because she's more religious then I am. But she knows how I feel, and I know how she feels. We find ways of patching up these differences just as we find ways of mending the problems we face that are related to culture, finances, politics, you name it." These types of participants generally inferred that their nominal interest in religion played a role in their decision to become involved in an inter-Christian marriage, as well as their decision to remain in an inter-Christian marriage.

When Faith and/or Ethnicity Impacts One's Sense of Self

Participants also asserted that both their ethnic and, or religious attachments were of central importance to their sense of identity, and the act of converting to Greek Orthodoxy was equated to loosing an important part of themselves. "Thinking about conversion is like thinking about uprooting something that is central to who you are, in my case, my Panamanian-Catholic background. In a sense, for a person like myself who has strong ethnic roots and religious roots, becoming Greek Orthodox feels as if I am opting to become a slightly different person, with a different mentality. So I stay where I am, and how I grew up, because that makes me feel comfortable. My religious and ethnic background is at the root of who I am. You just can't take these roots out and say, we're going to put you in another place. If I were to change or convert, I personally feel that I would be a different person."

A Renunciation of One's Faith Tradition

Converting to another faith tradition was conceptualized by many participants as a type of "renunciation and betrayal" of their current belief system. The following observation is indicative of this: "About eight years ago I came to church with my husband and there was this man in front of the church converting from Catholicism to Orthodoxy, and the words he repeated during this service just made me grab the pew and squeeze so hard. He said, 'I cast away all errors and false doctrines I have held,' and later I talked to the Father about that, and he said, 'I don't remember that,' but I do. These words echoed in my head, 'I cast away.' How can I cast away or in effect renounce what I was born with, what my family has been for generations? How can I renounce that? I can't. I can't."

A Betrayal and Disloyalty of One's Familial Culture

In other instances, several participants' paralleled conversion with the act of "betrayal" and disloyalty to their culture, family, parents, or grandparents. Some typical responses shared are as follows:

> "I really feel strongly about being Greek Orthodox, and to a large extent that's probably because my family is Greek. Conversion would make me feel like I have been disloyal to my family and who they are."
>
> "My family is Irish-Catholic and I feel that I should be Irish-Catholic. Converting would somehow seem as if I was betraying my family and ethnic roots."
>
> "My family has been a good Southern family who have been Church of Christ people for as long as anyone can remember. Converting would feel as if I was doing something wrong – almost like renouncing what you are – if you know what I mean."

A Respect for Extended Family Members' Feelings

A concern not to upset or insult extended families was repeatedly mentioned as a factor that discouraged conversion. These participants frequently stated that if they opted to convert, they feared that this decision might somehow hurt a parent(s) and, or their grandparents. One respondent's remarks illustrate this. "My mother is still alive. It's not that I participate as a Protestant anymore, because I attend the Greek Church with my family. But maybe subconsciously I feel as if converting would hurt her."

Respect for family member's feelings was often mentioned as either being equally important, or in some cases, more important than the notion of being a one-faith family. "My husband knows how I feel about converting, and he's grown to respect my thoughts and feelings.... Even though he's the religious one, he knows that my family's feelings are important, and I could never let them down by converting to his Church, even though it makes perfect sense in some ways."

Growing up in an Inter-Christian Household

Some participants mentioned that they had been raised in an inter-Christian home environment that was both stable and happy. These individuals concluded that their positive family-of-origin experiences had made it easier for them to choose to enter and remain in an inter-Christian marriage. One such respondent stated, "I grew up in an intermarried household. My father was Greek Orthodox and my mother was Catholic. My parents got along really well, and I have nothing but good happy memories of our home environment. So, when I considered getting married, I wasn't fazed by the fact that we weren't going to belong to the same religion."

Minimal Pressure From Family of Origin

When spouses perceived that their family of origin did not strongly resist their decision to intermarry, participants indicated it was easier for them to choose to enter an inter-Christian marriage. "If I had gotten the kind of flack from my family that some of the people tonight have described, I might have thought twice about marrying someone from another religion. But my parents were not very concerned about this, so long as she was Christian. As long as she was Christian, it didn't matter. So it was kind of easy for us to ignore the religious issue and just get married."

Conversion is a Personal, Private Issue

Participants generally ascribed to the notion that one's religious preference is more of a personal decision and less of a couple's decision. Participants' comments also frequently alluded to the serious nature of this decision, and observed that conversion should not be considered an option simply to satisfy the church, their extended families, or their spouse. Conversion must be heartfelt and God-inspired, otherwise future resentments and regrets might develop which could serve to negatively impact the well-being of the marriage. One respondent stated, "My husband is Catholic, but he comes to church with us. And I respect him, and I thank God that we can pray together, and we come to church together as a family. And I respect what is right for him… I want the best for my husband. And I pray to God that he will do what is right for him, and that God will direct all of us."

Imposing Conversion on One's Partner is Against God's will

It was not uncommon for participants to assert that they believed it was God's will that they respect each other's religious and cultural differences. Moreover, a failure to do so was interpreted as disrespectful, unholy behavior. The following brief exchange from several participants in one focus group illustrates this point.

"And I have this feeling, sometimes very strong, that I would love for him to convert. But the Lord brought him into this world a Catholic. So, who am I to push my husband to convert to my church – as beautiful and wonderful as I think it is. So, I don't push him to convert, but sometimes I think,… well, maybe I should, and we'd be better off. But then I just don't feel that's my place." Others in the group added their comments.

"I feel the same way."

"I think it should be their decision."

"I think it's a personal thing."

"Right. One between him and God."

"Yeah, that's right."

A Broad, Inclusive View of Their World

Intermarried couples' broad, inclusive perceptions of their world also appeared to affect how they viewed conversion and single-church marriage. Participants frequently stated that they belonged to a global society that was not nearly as compartmentalized as it once was. Therefore, as a result of this inclusive perception of the world, intermarried couples often place less value on conversion and the notion of a single-church marriage and family. While reflecting on the issue of conversion, one respondent stated. "In my mind, most of the differences between denominations are political and historical more than anything else. Even though my husband is Catholic and I am Greek Orthodox, I believe that we are both part of the same Christian faith. So I don't really see the need, except maybe for the sacraments. But my husband is Catholic, and receives in the Catholic Church.... The world is getting smaller, and we have to stop compartmentalizing each other. I believe it's the Christian thing to do."

Dominant American Societal and Cultural Influences

Since inter-Christian marriage is socially acceptable in our dominant American culture, and is perceived as working, these observations also appeared to provide spouses with two additional compelling motivations to ignore the value of conversion. Quoting from one participant, "We live in different times. The world has shrunk, and people are marrying outside of their groups with more frequency. So that's why I married my wife, and we weren't too concerned about our different religious and ethnic backgrounds. Besides that, just look around at all the intermarriages here. I think there are more of those than there are of the other type."

Age and Number of Years Married

Research has shown that as people age, their view of life tends to be less malleable and they tend to be less inclined to make big changes in their lives. Some research on intermarriage has also indicated that the longer couples remain intermarried, the less probable it is that such couples will become single-church couples. Observations from this study supported this, and also suggested that both age and length of time married might function to deter thoughts of conversion. From a respondent, "We've been able to share our two religions to our own satisfaction and our family's satisfaction and our spiritual satisfaction, so now we're content to go along that road after nearly fifteen years. Besides, at my age, I'm not interested in any big changes, and neither is my wife."

Additional Relevant Factors Related to Non-Orthodox Participants

There were other reasons that were also mentioned with less frequency. These reasons have been lumped together and are listed below.

Some non-Orthodox stated that they had not considered conversion because they were not convinced that Orthodoxy was any better than their own faith tradition.

Others suggested that they had not converted to Greek Orthodoxy because the Greek Orthodox Church they attended had failed to convince them it was interested in having them become part of the Orthodox Church. In these instances, it appeared that some participants might have considered conversion if the subject was broached in a respectful manner.

More information about Greek Orthodoxy also seemed key to non-Orthodox participants with regards to conversion. While many stated that they would likely not convert if given more information, a small but significant number stated that they might consider conversion more seriously if they knew more about Greek Orthodoxy.

Language and cultural differences were also mentioned as factors that prevented some non-Orthodox from considering conversion. These respondents appeared to suggest that language and cultural differences prevented them from feeling as if they could ever really feel like full members of the Greek Orthodox Church.

One final observation, while many non-Orthodox participants had chosen not to convert for one or more of the reasons mentioned above, several also stated that they came to our Churches regularly, were committed to these Churches, and felt like members of these Churches.

Summary

Some couples in this study appeared to practice two different faith traditions, while in other instances spouses belonged to two different faith traditions but were essentially practicing one faith tradition, generally Greek Orthodoxy. While many of these participants' remarks tended to lament the fact that they could not worship and/or belong to the same cultural and faith tradition, they reported being willing to accept their religious and cultural differences for one or more of the following reasons.

Conversion was not considered a viable option by intermarried couples because,...

- Spouses were more familiar with their own religious tradition
- Spouses were unfamiliar with their partner's religious tradition
- Doctrinal differences seemed difficult to accept
- Spouses had a high levels of attachment to their cultural heritage
- Spouses with equally low levels of religiosity had little interest in conversion
- One of the two spouses was nominally religious and had little interest in conversion
- Faith and/or ethnicity was perceived as being important to one or both spouses' sense of self
- Conversion was associated with a renunciation of one's faith tradition
- Conversion seemed like a betrayal and disloyalty to their familial culture
- Spouses sought to respect key extended family members' feelings

• Their positive family of origin experiences in an inter-Christian household promoted the idea of intermarriage

• Spouses received minimal pressure from their family of origin

• Conversion was perceived as a personal, private issue

• The notion of imposing conversion on one's partner was viewed as being against God's will

• Spouses espoused a broad, inclusive view of the world that seemed to promote intermarriage

• Dominant American societal and cultural influences encouraged intermarriage

• Age and the number of years that spouses were married seemed to discourage thoughts of conversion

Chapter Five

Reasons Why Intermarried Couples Become Single-church Couples[37]

While moderating a focus group in the Northeast, a participant made the following comments: "I'm one of those non-Greek Orthodox who's been straddling the fence for a long time regarding conversion. A few Sundays back, my son comes up to me – he's seven now – and he says, 'Dad I'd like to stay home from church today with you. Can you talk to Mom?' Well, I'll tell you this was a wake-up call for me. I knew right then and there I needed to make some adjustments, otherwise my son might end up without much religion."

Several respondents described having one of these *"aha!"* moments with regards to the issue of conversion. These were instances that prompted individuals to reassess their intermarried situation. Some of these instances were like revelations, and were the result of certain individual, marital and family changes that had taken place since they decided to enter into an inter-Christian marriage.

Others described this decision more in terms of a long process that seemed to be leading them toward conversion due to a number of interrelated experiences. One respondent stated, "I've been thinking about conversion for a long time now. I guess it's the result of many things. I'm not there yet, but I think one day soon I will be."

However the change in attitude might have taken place, some research indicates that up to 40-50% of all intermarried couples will eventually become single-churchcouples.[38] Moreover, while one of the objectives of the IRP was not to study conversion rates among intermarried couples in the GOA, results clearly indicated that many participants (11%) were considering conversion for one or more of the following reasons.

Conversion Eliminates Possible Sources of Contention

Results from the IRP suggest that a small but sizable number of intermarried spouses believe that conversion can positively impact their marriage. In these cases, these spouses were leaning toward conversion and asserted that conversion would likely strengthen their marriage by removing possible sources of contention that could compromise spousal and extended family stability.

Time, Tolerance, and Education

Time, tolerance and education classes appeared to be invaluable toward helping intermarried couples decide if they should become single-faith couples. "What I needed was some space to make the decision," stated one respondent who was embracing Orthodoxy in the near future. "In my heart of hearts, I always knew that I would convert, but if someone had pressured me, that wouldn't have been good." These spouses stated that if they felt forced, manipulated, or made to feel guilty, they imagined that these types of tactics would have proven counterproductive to the conversion process

Respectfully Sharing Greek Orthodoxy

If a non-Orthodox spouse is approached respectfully and sincerely with the idea of conversion, and if the individual approached discerns that they are not being proselytized, this evangelical approach can facilitate conversion. For example, one participant stated, "I never forced him. It was his decision. I respected him and knew if I had tried to push, that would have been harmful to our marriage. It was his decision, not mine. He was the one that had to feel like that's what God wanted for our family."

Weak Religious and Ethnic Connections

A weak connection to one's religious tradition, together with a renewed sense of the importance of religion, made it easier for some participants to consider conversion. "I wasn't very religious when we first got married. As you get older, and your priorities change, religion seemed to take on more importance for me. Since my wife and kids are Greek Orthodox, it seemed like a natural thing for me to consider the Orthodox Church more seriously. Today I am in the process of going through the Inquirer's Class to enter the Orthodox Church."

Similarly, a weak connection to one's religious tradition, along with the perception that conversion might strengthen one's marriage and enhance one's relationship with one's in-laws also offered enough incentive to consider conversion. For instance, one respondent said, "The main reason why we got married in the Orthodox Church was because this decision was going to help our family. His parents didn't accept me easily because I was previously married, and so I said to myself, this is going to be my mother-in-law, and I want to make this work. So we got married Orthodox, and now I'm considering conversion for some of the same reasons. Besides that, I really didn't have any strong connections to my religion."

It is important to also note, that evidence from the IRP suggests that some adult children who were born into and raised in a Greek Orthodox family, and were nominally religious, but had strong ethnic ties, ended up converting to their spouses' faith tradition. In these cases, they said that they would attend their partner's church and would periodically visit the Greek Orthodox Church in an effort to affiliate with their family and the Greek community.

The Arrival of Children

When intermarried couples decide to have children, or when their children begin to mature and begin asking questions about religion, many intermarried couples who have been worshipping in both partners' churches decide to attend one church. These couples remain intermarried. Others reconsider their decision to remain intermarried. In these instances, one partner considers conversion. For example, one father said, "I think that it's very important that the kids see both parents go to church.... When I would sit at home on Sundays, as the kids grew I began to hear the kids saying, 'why do I have to go, Dad isn't going.' So then, I began to rethink what I was doing, and started going to church regularly. And after a while, I also began thinking about maybe even converting."

A Love of Orthodoxy

Conversion that was coerced or entered into simply to satisfy church rules, the extended family, and/or one's spouse was repeatedly described in pejorative terms. As such, remarks like the following one were made repeatedly. "I feel very strongly about this. If you don't feel that you should convert — you shouldn't. And if you feel like you're being pressured, and you convert, what good is that? It might just lead to trouble in the future. What I mean is, the person who converts may end up being resentful." Conversely, having a sincere, heartfelt commitment to the Orthodox faith was perceived as another legitimate, justifiable, and healthy reason to convert.

Summary

Although most participants involved in the IRP appeared to be very comfortable with their decision to intermarry, there were a small number of participants in this study (11%) who were considering conversion. Intermarried couples considering this option were generally motivated to do so for one or more of the following reasons.

• Some spouses and couples believe that conversion eliminates possible sources of contention.

• Some individuals will eventually consider conversion if they are given ample time, their decision to intermarry is respected and tolerated and they receive some quality religious education.

• When priests and lay leaders respectfully share Greek Orthodoxy with non-Orthodox, this approach can facilitate conversion.

• When an individual has a weak religious and ethnic connection, this can prompt individuals to consider conversion.

• When the children arrive, some intermarried parents determine that their conversion is in the best interest of their children's religious development.

• Some individuals determine to convert because they develop a love for Orthodoxy.

Chapter Six

How Inter-christian Couples View Their Marriages[39]

Participants in this study were generally involved in functional, healthy marriages. Their remarks suggested that they loved one another, and worked hard toward ensuring that their marriages would not merely survive, but also thrive.

Despite the additional difficulties and challenges they faced as intermarried couples, the majority of those who participated in this study did not appear to have any major regrets with their decision to enter an inter-Christian marriage and remain intermarried. The following remarks were typical of most participants: "I have no regrets, and I wouldn't do it any other way. She has been the best thing that ever happened to me, and our love for one another has helped us make things work."

Although most couples did not view their religious and cultural differences as being especially more significant than other differences they faced, these couples were aware that their religious and cultural differences could potentially create marital conflict and they worked hard to make certain that these potential sources of conflict would not create strife in their marriages. "It's true," stated one respondent, "there are some extra challenges, but they haven't been anything we couldn't handle. It just takes a willingness to work things out."

Their competency at finding ways of resolving the challenges that emerged as a result of their religious and cultural differences appeared to be immensely important to their well-being. For instance, one religious spouse who was married to someone who "showed no interest in organized religion" lamented the fact that she attended church services alone on most Sundays, but almost in the same breath also remarked that she viewed this time as personal time that afforded her an opportunity "to be with God."

Most of these participants did not view their religious and cultural differences as serious threats to their marriages' stability. "I've seen other couples that have worse problems than we do as an intermarried couple. We know several Orthodox couples that have it worse. As far as I'm concerned, I think our marital happiness has a lot to do with the love and commitment we share with each other, and less to do with our religious and cultural differences." They often maintained that these differences were generally of no greater significance than other differences that they faced as couples. Most of these couples, especially the Baby Boomers, had long addressed their differences and found ways of either circumventing them or eliminating them. Even though many had managed to accept and learn to live with their differences, some still viewed these differences as potential sources of difficulty that needed periodic attention throughout the marital life cycle. Comments such as "this is a work in progress," and "there are plenty of ways to create problems in a mixed marriage" and, "you've got to make the best of things," served to reinforce the need for continued vigilance.

Spouses also repeatedly maintained that their religious and cultural diversity functioned to enrich their lives as individuals and couples. Comments such as "it's an enriching arrangement," and "I feel richer and not poorer" were generally used to describe their marriages. Numerous participants observed that their partner's religious tradition provided them with another dimension of Christianity that served to broaden and stretch their perception of their own religious tradition. One respondent stated the following while reflecting on his inter-Christian, intercultural marriage: "We both draw upon very rich traditions, and within each of our traditions there are many, many good moments to build upon. This has certainly broadened our understanding of our own and each other's religions tradition." Many participants also described how their partner's ethnic heritage added cultural richness and variety to their lives. The following observations attest to this: "Two Easter baskets are better than one," and, "The different foods, languages, traditions and religious perspectives are more enriching than belonging to one faith and one culture. The diversity is the beauty of intermarriage. That's precisely what makes them kind of special"

Their love for one another, their desire to see their marriages succeed, their interest in maintaining family stability, their respect for diversity, and their tolerant and patient attitudes for their respective religious and cultural differences appeared to be indispensable to their efforts to advance marital and family satisfaction and stability.

The Downside of Being Intermarried

Although most intermarried couples involved in the IRP viewed their intermarriages in fundamentally positive terms, some respondents did indicate that their religious and cultural differences tended to create a wedge between them. The fact that couples were raised and belonged to different cultural and faith traditions tended to create a low to moderate sense of distance between some participants. "It's been a challenge, and I sometimes feel an emptiness at times when I'm at church alone. And this emptiness, I think, is from feeling a bit distant from my family in this part of our lives."

Couples with equally strong commitments to their faith tradition were especially challenged by their religious differences. They maintained that their religious differences could be detrimental to their marriage. Because religion was an integral part of their self-identity, worldview and daily schedules, their religious differences had the potential to create varying degrees of distance and separation between them. "It's been a challenge, I won't deny it. We're both very faithful, and we both want to practice our faiths rigorously and with regular involvement. So, when I started going to the Greek Church, I got rather resentful and frustrated because it just wasn't the same and I felt deprived of something very important. And this really affected us for a while and I wondered what the consequences of this would be until I found a way to meet my own spiritual needs."

Similarly, some spouses' ethnic differences were also described in divisive terms. "I'm one of those Americans who've been here so long that when people ask me what my ethnic background is, I tell them that 'I'm just American.' Anyway, when I met my wife, I suppose one of the things that attracted me to her was the fact that she had an ethnic identity.... Most of the time our cultural differences haven't created too many problems. But there have been times when either she's tried to push too much ethnicity on me and I've resented it, or when I've been insensitive to her needs to express this side of herself when we've had some serious problems."

Inter-Christian but not Inter-Religious

Inter-Christian marriages were generally accepted and viewed in a positive light, but inter-religious marriages involving non-Christians were generally viewed in a negative light. When participants were asked if they might have considered a non-Christian spouse, most believed that the differences were "too great" and the potential problems from these differences might be problematic to couple and family well-being. "My Christian faith is important to me, and so I feel that it was important that I find a Christian to marry. Otherwise, how could either I or my future wife have continued to grow spiritually in a marriage where both partners belong to a different religion?"

There appeared to be a general consensus among respondents that they would not consider entering an inter-religious marriage, since the religious and cultural differences in such relationships are greater than they could tolerate. Such marriages were also perceived as possessing certain unbridgeable marital and family challenges. "It's been hard enough sometimes to be from different Christian traditions," stated one respondent. "I can't fathom being married to a non-Christian, and dealing with the difficulties our differences would create. I think that would simply be too much difference to deal with."

They also reasoned that such a decision might disturb their parents and negatively impact their children's perception of religion and culture. "Besides the couple difficulties," stated another participant, "I think extended family difficulties and the challenges of raising children might be intolerable. I just don't see how you can raise children to be religious in an inter-religious home. And besides, I don't even think that my parents would have blessed such a marriage."

Participants also stated that they imagined that one's level of commitment to one's faith tradition might influence one's decision to intermarry across religious lines. They further stated that nominally committed Christians would likely be more prone to entering an inter-religious marriage with someone outside of the Christian faith tradition. One participant with a low level of religiosity stated, "I'm not a very religious person, so if I happened to fall in love with — say, a Jewish person or a Muslim person, I might have considered marriage to them if other things were right."

Summary

- Intermarried couples generally view their marriages in positive terms.
- They generally believe that their different ethnic and religious backgrounds enrich their lives as well as their children's lives.
- Some spouses encounter challenges related to their cultural and religious differences that can potentially undermine individual, couple and family well-being.
- Many couples with high ethnic and religious attachments were the most likely to encounter the serious challenges. These couples were generally able to find a mutually satisfying resolution to their challenges without outside intervention.
- Inter-Christian couples that have a moderate to high attachment to Christianity do not consider inter-religious marriage as a viable option. Because of their religious attachments, they believe that interreligious marriages could create insurmountable marital and family challenges.

Chapter Seven

A View of Intermarriage in the GOA

As I travel around the country doing marriage building retreats and seminars, I have come to understand that inter-Christian, intercultural marriages are very complex human systems that often encounter a host of developmental and social ecological challenges. The next several chapters will explain what I mean.

I would like to begin by featuring two different couples. These short illustrations will reveal some of the complexity and challenges that inter-Christian couples encounter. Each couple will be at different stages in the marital and family life cycles. This means that they will be grappling with different (a) individual, (b) couple, (c) family and extended family challenges. I want to also ask you to pay close attention to both the developmental challenges, as well as the social ecological challenges they are seeking to negotiate – both of these concepts will become more familiar to you as you read on. But before meeting these couples, I want to introduce you to an approach that can help you understand most of the complex challenges these spouses, couples and families face.

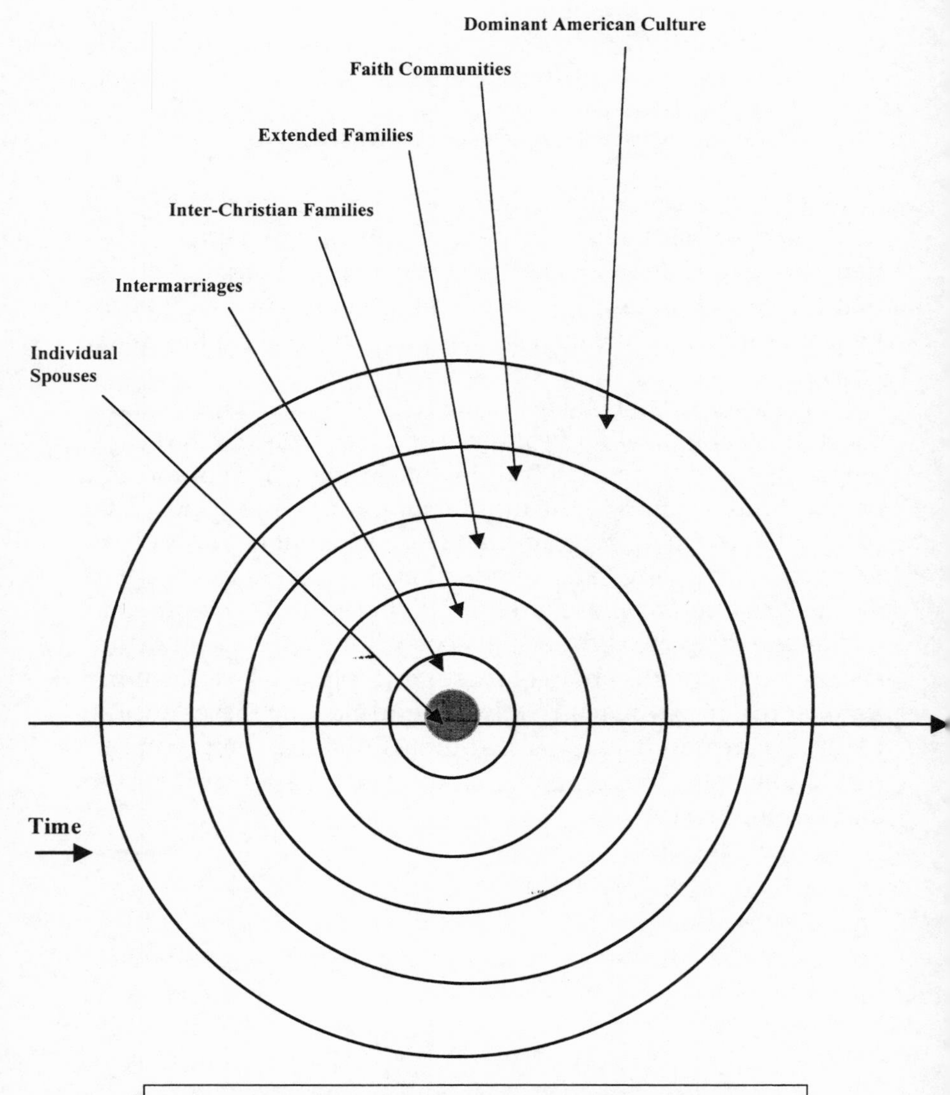

An Orthodox Social Ecological Developmental Theory

A Theory of Intermarriages in the GOA

Social science theories function to organize and explain human behavior. They do not represent the truth with a capital "T," but simply afford us a way to interpret and understand the complex human and social behavior we are observing.

The figure shown is a graphic example of a theory that can help you in your efforts to minister to the intermarried couples and families worshipping in the churches you serve. It emerged from the Interfaith Research Project (IRP) and is entitled, A Developmental Social Ecological Theory of Intermarriages in the Greek Orthodox Archdiocese of America.[40] Let me explain how this theory might prove useful to you.

Warning! At this point I suspect that some of you might be tempted to skip to the next section. Please don't. That is because the rest of the chapter – together with the next four chapters – will require you to understand the next few paragraphs.

The Developmental Dimension

A cursory glance at the figure will reveal an arrow. Underneath the arrow you will see the word TIME. This part of the diagram illustrates the maturation process we are constantly passing through as individuals, couples and families. Social scientists have helped us understand the developmental process from conception through death. They have termed this process the *life cycle*, and identified certain distinctive stages of development. Infancy, adolescence and middle age are words that we use to refer to these stages.

Family scholars have also identified stages that marriages and families pass through. Just as individuals pass through a life cycle, they have pointed out that marriages and families also pass through a life cycle with distinct stages. The descriptors, newlyweds, families with young children and families with adolescents are examples of some of the stages in the marital and family life cycle. This chapter will be concerned with identifying some of the challenges that intermarried spouses, couples and their families encounter as they and their children mature.

The Social Ecological Dimension

In addition, social scientists have helped us acquire a keener understanding of the way that our social environment impacts us as individuals, couples and families. They have pointed out that we are all embedded in a sophisticated social ecology that profoundly influences the way we think and act. The circles in the figure function to illustrate this observation.

IRP focus group participants were asked to respond to the following question: What is it like being intermarried? They repeatedly alluded to the social subsystems depicted in the above diagram in their efforts to describe their individual, couple and family lived experiences and challenges. As such, the information that follows will also describe how intermarried spouses' and couples' social environment impacted individual, marital and family stability and well-being.

By understanding the materials in this chapter, I believe you will develop an even deeper appreciation for the unique challenges that this growing population of faithful encounter. Moreover, I would argue that together with our Greek Orthodox foundation, a good understanding of this theory and the information that follows will help you minister more effectively to this growing population of faithful. A good understanding of this theory should also assist you in your efforts to help your congregations become more sensitive to the unique challenges that intermarried couples and their families encounter: to God's glory and the continuation of His holy work.

Balancing Individual and Couple Needs – Meet Martha and Gus

Martha (31) and Gus (33) have been married for about eight years. Martha is Mexican Catholic of Mexican decent and Gus is Greek Orthodox. Gus considers himself nominally religious, but is firmly connected to his ethnic background. Martha has higher levels of religious commitment and an equally high level of connection to her ethnic background.

Almost from the beginning of their marriage, this couple admits to having constantly and unsuccessfully argued about their religious and cultural differences. Issues such as where they should worship, their future children's names, where they should baptize, and which ethnic and religious traditions they should include in their family life have remained unresolved.

One day, out of frustration, Gus unilaterally decides that the couple should belong to the Greek Orthodox Church. He thus submits a pledge to St. Nicholas Greek Orthodox Church. When Martha hears about this, she becomes angry and resentful because she views herself as "the religious one." She confronts Gus, and demands an explanation. In response, Gus retorts, "I'm Greek, and I can't deny that about myself any longer." He also refuses to engage in further conversation. Martha becomes angrier and makes some derogatory remarks about his background. Gus leaves the house, and does not return for several hours. By then, Martha's interest in arguing wanes, but her resentment lingers. Gus is somewhat relieved because he does not have to hear Martha yell, but he remains discouraged over their religious and cultural differences. The couple fails to address this issue again.

The residual effects of this encounter and others like it are that Martha celebrates most religious feast days alone. Moreover, both spouses also tend to celebrate ethnic holidays with extended families and apart from one another. Their decision to start a family is also postponed. Neither feels comfortable having children until they feel better about their marriage and where the children will be baptized.

Some Observations

Participants from the IRP frequently stated that their religious and ethnic connections fulfilled numerous spiritual, moral, psychological, and social needs at a personal level. Moreover, these individual needs were often described as being compelling and important enough to cause them to find ways of fulfilling these needs. Respondents also stated that if they desired marital stability and satisfaction, they could not simply consider their own personal religious and cultural needs to the exclusion of their partner's needs in their efforts to cultivate a healthy, functional marriage. Furthermore, to the extent that participants were successful in striking a balance between their personal and marital needs, couples were able to meet their personal religious and cultural needs, as well as achieving marital stability and satisfaction. When spouses either ignored their own needs, their partner's needs, or their relationship's needs, then one or both spouses would generally experience some internal conflict which often translated into some external marital and family instability and dissatisfaction. Given these observations, what can be stated about the challenges that Gus and Martha appear to be encountering?

First, both spouses appear to have certain definite religious and ethnic needs.

Second, the strategy they have employed to meet their personal needs has had a toxic effect on (a) individual well-being, (b) couple stability and satisfaction, and (c) their plans to start a family.

Third, this couple appears to be caught in an unresolved stalemate. Moreover, the longer they remain stuck, the greater the likelihood more damage will be inflicted on their individual, marital and family well-being.

Fourth, these challenges seem to have a negative impact on their religious and spiritual development as individuals and as a couple. Their efforts to cultivate a Christian home environment are also stymied, as are their efforts to celebrate their ethnic backgrounds.

If this couple could be helped to see what is occurring between them, there may be a possibility that individual and couple satisfaction could be improved. Specifically, if they could be helped to see that in their efforts to meet their personal religious and cultural needs, they have ignored their needs as a couple, this could give them a different perspective of the frustrations and discontent they are experiencing. In addition, if this couple can be convinced to strike a balance between their needs as individuals and a couple, chances are good that the stalemate will be resolved.

Balancing Nuclear Family Needs With Extended Family Needs

Balancing nuclear family needs and extended family needs is a skill that couples must also master. When couples are unsuccessful in accomplishing this task, individual, couple, nuclear family and extended family well-being can suffer. The following example illustrates how this can happen.

John and Mary

John (27) and Mary (25) have been married for about one year. John is a first generation Greek Orthodox Christian, and Mary is a non-practicing Roman Catholic from a mixed ethnic background. This couple is happily married, but also admits to encountering some serious challenges. Some of the reasons to account for this last statement are chronicled below.

When they began dating, John's parents were quick to point out that "it was fine that you date a non-Greek for fun and games sake, but you should only permit yourself to become serious with a Greek girl, since marriages with non-Greeks do not work out." John politely listened to his parents, but because of his increasing affection for Mary, he quickly found that he could not respect his parent's advice and continued to date her. John was also determined to hide his parent's dissatisfaction from Mary, fearing that if he shared this information, it would somehow compromise their relationship. Even though John hid his parent's displeasure, Mary sensed his parents' disapproval, and remained mildly concerned but failed to broach the subject with John fearing the negative consequences of such a conversation.

Several months passed, and they became very serious. John proposed marriage, and Mary accepted. The next day, John decided to share this news with his parents privately. This is because he feared his parents would react negatively.

Predictably, they did not take the news well and they began to issue threats and ultimatums like the following, "We do not want her in our family. If you marry this girl, we will disown you." This was an ugly encounter that ended with these words from John as he stormed out of the house. "It's my life and I don't care what you both say. If you want to disown me, so be it. I love this girl, and will marry her, with or without your consent." He would not come home for several weeks.

After a cooling off period, his parents began to notice that they might lose contact with their son. As such, their tone softened, they made contact with John and indicated that they would tolerate his decision, if the "marriage would take place in the Greek Orthodox Church." They also indicated that they would "not be surprised if this marriage did not survive." Despite this last statement, John was satisfied with these concessions and contact was reestablished.

Since John knew that Mary was a non-practicing Catholic, he asked her if she would agree to get married in the Greek Orthodox Church, stating that "this would please his parents." He did not, however, share the full extent of his parent's reservations and disappointment with their decision to wed. Mary also failed to ask any detailed questions, even though she continued to be concerned about his parents' feelings toward her and their decision to wed.

Wishing to improve her rather distant and cold relationship with John's parents, Mary consented, and the couple was married in the Greek Orthodox Church. Unfortunately, to Mary's chagrin, after the marriage her in-laws continued to remain only distantly cordial toward her. About six months after the marriage, John's parents would approach him, strongly urging him to ask Mary to join the Greek Orthodox Church. "Where are your future children going to be baptized? You don't want them to get baptized in another church. Why don't you ask Mary to convert? This would please us greatly."

As a result of these and other similar remarks, John went home that night and awkwardly began making the following proposal, "I think we should have a family church – the Greek Church. It would also be nice if you thought about converting. I think this would be good for our future children." Dumbfounded and surprised at these sudden suggestions, Mary responded, "Where in the world has this come from John? You've never suggested to me that religion was important to you before this day. I don't know, that's a lot to think about."

Not wishing to disclose who prompted him to make this statement, John defensively responded, "So what's wrong with having a family church and being the same religion? And what's to think about. It's no big deal. We go once in a while and everyone's happy."

Upon hearing this last statement, Mary becomes visibly irritated, and says, "Now I get it. It's your parents who put you up to this. And now you're siding with them. Aren't you?" "And what if it's true?" John retorts defensively and with some irritation of his own."Do you know how that makes me feel when you talk to them about things that concern us, before you talk to me. It makes me feel betrayed, John. And another thing, how can I trust you, if I think you're withholding information or siding with them."

That night and the next several days would be filled with long, emotional, exhausting arguments and conversations. John would finally tell Mary the truth about his parents' feelings for them. He would also ask for her forgiveness, and promise never to withhold information from her again. Mary would also disclose her premarital fears and concerns regarding his parents' feelings toward her and ask for his forgiveness. The couple would also begin forming some new boundaries of the type that would not allow John's parents to divide them again.

Some Observations

Participants' comments from the IRP repeatedly observed that members from both partner's extended families have needs – particularly parents. For example, parents sometimes have a need to see their adult children married in their faith background. Parents may also desire that their married children and future grandchildren actively practice their religious and ethnic traditions. In an effort to meet these needs, parents may apply overt or covert pressure upon intermarried couples and families. As such, balancing nuclear family needs and extended family needs is a skill that young couples must master.

Similarly, participants also repeatedly stated that it was necessary for them to learn how to draw healthy boundaries between themselves and their extended families to protect their nuclear families from unwanted extended family intrusions. As couples learned how to love and honor their parents, while also drawing clear boundaries between themselves and their parents, this approach made things easier for everyone concerned.

Participants also observed that when intermarried couples were unsuccessful in drawing clear boundaries between themselves and their extended family, some respondents were forced to subordinate and, or ignore their nuclear family needs in an effort to meet extended families' expectations and needs. Furthermore, this decision tended to have a negative impact on marital satisfaction and nuclear family religious well-being.

In light of these observations, what can be stated about John and Mary? First, in John's desire to honor and attend to his parents' needs, he lost sight of Mary's needs, and his developing relationship's needs. These omissions distressed Mary, and created marital conflict. Second, while Mary's contributions are not as clear, a strong case could be made that she also made similar mistakes. Even though she sensed that John's parents were displeased, she did not request any clarification from John. All of which suggests that Mary's silence also inhibited this couple from meeting their individual and couple needs. Third, only after some serious discussion, is this couple able to make the necessary adjustments, and strike a balance between their individual needs, their needs as a couple and John's parent's needs. Until then, these needs remain unattended and serve to negatively impact both spouses.

Summary

I have counseled hundreds of intermarried spouses and couples from across the marital life cycle utilizing the information found in this resource. Many of these individuals and couples have expressed their gratitude, repeatedly stating that my observations had been very helpful. I think most pastors can have similar successes with this population if they incorporate the ideas and suggestions in this book into their work. With God's help, some knowledge of the unique challenges that these spouses, couples and families face, together with the assistance of this theory, I believe that the complex challenges that emerge in intermarried households can be opportunities for religious and spiritual growth. This information should help you guide conflicted spouses and couples away from the tendency that many may have to view their differences as deficits and threats to individual, couple and family well-being[41].

The next several chapters will continue building upon the information presented in this chapter. As you acquaint yourself with this information, the additional knowledge and insights you gain should be helpful to many souls[42].

Chapter Eight

Challenges Facing Dating Couples

> "When we were dating, I was having some serious problems with my husband John's family. They seemed so cold and unwelcoming. John suggested that I make an appointment with his priest Father Jim to discuss this, so I did. When we met, I hardly gave him an opportunity to introduce himself when I asked, 'Are all Greek families so unwelcoming?' After Father Jim stopped laughing, he assured me that Greek Americans were generally warm and welcoming. He also went ahead and offered me some very helpful advice about Greek families and the dating process. This discussion made a big difference for me, and to this day I remain very grateful. If it wasn't for his counsel, John and I might not have gotten married."
>
> Focus Group Participant

This chapter will focus upon some of the chief dating challenges that young adults face who consider intermarriage.[43] In Chapter 9 I will concentrate on the challenges related to the engagement period, Chapter 10 will discuss newlywed challenges and Chapter 11 will consider the remainder of the marital and family life cycle.

General Dating Challenges

As young adults approach their early twenties, most are busy creating a life apart from their family of origin. During this process, the parent/child relationship is changing. Both parents and their young adult children are learning how to interrelate as adults. Young adults are also busy developing careers and forming new relationships. Marriage also begins to become a consideration. Forming intimate relationships with the opposite sex through the dating process becomes one of the defining tasks of this stage.

Dating affords young adults the opportunity to get to know the opposite sex better. As they meet and date a variety of people, young adults will hopefully begin to identify some of the traits they desire in a partner. This process will generally also help dating partners get to know themselves better.

In addition to the usual dating challenges that most couples encounter, inter-Christian and intercultural dating couples can expect to encounter challenges related to their religious and cultural differences – especially when the dating process evolves and becomes serious. The following challenges are typical of what they might encounter. They are offered here – together with some commentary – because time and again participants' comments from the IRP indicated that they experienced certain challenges that created personal and family misery and heartache. These participants also frequently stated that they might have benefited from some helpful counsel as they encountered these unexpected challenges. "I'm not saying that I would have talked to Fr. George," stated one respondent. "I'm only saying that I would have appreciated some advice from someone when I was dating my wife. There were some things that happened related to religious differences that really made things hard."

Typical Individual Challenges

If you were to talk to a typical young adult today, he or she would tell you that they hope to marry one day. They might then proceed to describe a rather bleak view of marriage. Given the divorce culture in which we live, together with the fact that many of their parents divorced, most would be pessimistic about long-term marriages. They would also likely share their doubts about ever successfully finding a partner for life.[44]

Many young adults are confused about marriage today. Not only are they influenced by their own fears and experiences, but they have also been profoundly impacted by postmodern, secular views of marriage that are essentially self-centered[45]. Also, this is a time when hormones are coursing through their veins and they are influenced by idyllic notions of love.

In the midst of all these potentially destructive and distracting influences, young adults are dating and making decisions about their future. So, it is fair to suggest that one challenge they will face is related to their efforts to sort through their feelings and thoughts while also taking an inventory of what they desire out of life.

In many instances, thoughts related to the importance of religion and culture are ignored as irrelevant or insignificant. This is true despite the fact that human scientists inform us that religion and culture are both central determinants as to how people think and view the world. So, while most young adults might not necessarily construe religion and culture as an important consideration before marriage, after marriage many will look back retrospectively and indicate that they should have spent more time considering these issues. A respondent stated, "I really wish I had thought more about these matters when I was dating. I think it would have spared both me and my husband a lot of grief, because we've had a lingering disagreement about the importance of religion and culture over the years."

Finding ways to help young adults embrace the importance of religion and culture is a task that pastors and lay leaders must accept. This is especially true of religion; since our secular society does not help young adults take a personal inventory of how important their religious background might be to them.

Typical Extended Family Challenges

Parents may politely tolerate their adult children's dating partners until the dating process moves from a casual to a more serious level. If they are unhappy with their adult child's choice, they may then seek to undermine the dating process when couples become serious by showing displeasure and threatening to withhold their blessings. One Greek Orthodox participant stated, "It wasn't so bad at the beginning when we first started dating. My folks sort of tolerated the situation, although I knew they were displeased because they'd make remarks like, 'You know, she's not Greek. You should find a Greek girl.' Circumstances really began heating up when we started getting serious. There were numerous arguments and some ugly things said on both sides. They even threatened to disown me."

In most instances, respondents in the focus groups stated that the reason why parents may have negative reactions is linked to one or more of these factors: (1) they are recent new comers to this country and are more likely to be influenced by old world values, (2) they are concerned for their adult child's future well-being, (3) they construe their adult child's decision to become intimately involved with an outsider as disrespectful and potentially damaging to the family's reputation.

It is important to mention that while some tension typically emerges between the dating couple and their extended families, this tension generally begins to lift when parents discern that their displeasure and threats have failed. Cutoffs between adult children and parents are thus generally avoided because parents and children do not want to lose touch with each other. New and healthy boundaries eventually emerge to meet (a) the individual dating partners' needs, (b) the couple's needs, and (c) both extended families' needs.

Guidelines That Should Assist Clergy and Lay Church Workers

• Whether a priest or lay leader utilizes the above information one-on-one or in a group setting is irrelevant. Finding ways of sharing and discussing these challenges – along with the other challenges listed in subsequent chapters – should prove beneficial to teens and young adults alike. Along with the occasional individual pastoral counseling session, Sunday School, adult education classes, GOYA and YAL encounters are other ideal venues where this information could be introduced and discussed.

• Should a young adult or couple approach you for some counsel related to the dating challenges they are experiencing, you might be tempted to respond in one of two ways. Some might be inclined to dismiss their plea and assume a hands-off approach; others might end up owning the problem and seeking to resolve it. Both approaches are flawed and can potentially create some pastoral problems. Instead, here are some guidelines that should assist you.

• Interpret the individual or couple's presence as an opportunity that can facilitate personal and couple religious and spiritual growth.

• Listen carefully and respectfully, and do not offer your observations immediately. Even though most young adults' stories are remarkably similar, all tend to be different because of the blend of unique personalities that are involved.

• In general, if dating couples approach a clergyman or lay leader for some advice, it is because they have passed the casual dating stage and are involved in a serious dating relationship. During the course of your discussion, you also might consider encouraging such individuals or couples to consider how their religious and cultural differences might challenge them in the future should they consider engagement and marriage. (Remember to refer these couples to the couple's resource *When You Intermarry*, and especially to Chapter 12 entitled, *The Value of Premarital Preparation*. This chapter will help them isolate their challenges, while the remainder of the resource, together with your own expertise should help them find some resolution to their differences.)

• Remind the individual or couple that if they take the time to inventory their religious and cultural needs, this approach will pay dividends in the future. Let them also know that even though their religious and cultural differences may not seem important at this stage of the life cycle, should they decide to become intermarried, they will likely encounter some challenges that could have a negative impact on individual, couple and family well-being.

• You might also ask if the individual or couple has considered the benefits of entering a single-churchmarriage as opposed to considering an interchurch marriage. In this case, take special precaution to try and remain objective. Most individuals or couples in our society generally do not want someone, even clergy, giving them specific advice about personal matters. (For guidance and some suggestions as to how to proceed at this point consider the information under *The Pros and Cons of Intermarriage* in Chapter 9.)

• Throughout this process, you should make it clear that you are neither endorsing nor objecting to the idea of intermarriage, but are simply offering information as a way to assist the young adult or couple in their efforts to make some decisions and resolve their present challenge(s). If red flags appear while this process is unfolding that are suggestive of future individual, marital and family difficulties, your observations should be prefaced with statements such as the following one: "If I were you, I might take a more careful look at…."

• As you listen, please also keep in mind that the less complex challenges you will hear will be inherently related to either (1) individual needs, (2) couple needs or, (3) extended family pressure. (For more information and some illustrations regarding this last statement, review Chapter 7 again. This chapter provides two case studies utilizing the above theory. This theory should assist the couple in negotiating some of the pitfalls associated with extended families during the dating process.)

• The challenges that seem to contain conflicting levels of individual, couple and extended family needs will be the most complicated and hardest to resolve. That is because of the different levels of conflicting subsystem needs. (For more information about this last point, please consult Chapter 7 which discusses this subject in greater detail.) Suggesting the resource for intermarried couples is also a good way to begin assisting these individuals or couples. Chapter 8 in this resource entitled, *Acquiring a Better Understanding of the Unique Challenges Faced by Intermarried Couples* should prove helpful. Of course, such advice will require you to familiarize yourself with this chapter.

• Meaningful advice from scripture, sharing your own personal pastoral experiences, as well as offering frequent reminders that he or she is in God's hands will prove immensely helpful. In most instances, a supportive ear and some spiritual counsel is all that is needed. If circumstances degenerate, and you feel as if you are dealing with an issue that is beyond your own expertise, you should determine to consult with your bishop, another priest, lay leader or refer the individual to a professional psychotherapist in whom you trust.[46]

• In conjunction with this last point, please remember that research indicates that people with personal problems will seek their pastor's assistance first or early on.[47] Other studies also indicate that people afflicted with a serious mental illness are as likely to approach their pastor as a mental health worker.[48] As such, it is important that clergy need to educate themselves about mental illness and marital and family dysfunction while also understanding their limitations and knowing when to refer.[49]

An Exercise for the GOYA and YAL

Most young people in the community you serve will likely not solicit your observations regarding the information contained in this chapter. So, you must find ways of introducing them to this material. That is because, even though young adults will not seek this information out, respondents involved in the IRP repeatedly stated that they would have benefited from it. The GOYA and YAL groups in the parish are ideal ways to present these materials to your teens and young adults.

Using this type of proactive approach should prove beneficial to the adolescents and young adults in your community.

This information will help them in either their present or future dating relationships. Naturally, the approach you take with the GOYA will be slightly different than the approach you take with the YAL. Teens will generally not be thinking in serious terms about long-term relationships, So, some of this information will not be as meaningful to them and you will have to struggle a bit to reach them. Remember this, my experience working with teens has taught me that even though they may seem disinterested, this does not mean they are. Most will be listening. Conversely, young adults will likely be receptive to conversations related to serious dating relationships, engagement and marriage. Therefore, you should find it easier to generate conversation with this group. Pastors and other church workers thinking about presenting the information in this chapter, together with other information related to intermarriage may find the following observations and questions useful.

There are many ways to utilize these questions. So, be creative. You know your young people better than I do. For example, in some instances a round table discussion or panel discussion may prove helpful. In other instances, recruiting a speaker who is familiar with these materials who can discuss premarital concerns may be a better approach. However, in all cases the process should allow for some meaningful exchange between those in attendance as well as some prayerful counsel. Care should also be taken to cultivate a safe environment where all questions and concerns can be broached and discussed respectfully. If participants do not feel safe, the quality of the conversation will suffer. During this encounter, here are some questions of central importance that you should consider covering. Depending on the level of interaction among those in attendance, you will need somewhere between one or two sessions to address these questions and the concerns connected to them.

- Did you know that over 70% of Greek Orthodox young adults intermarry?

• Do you think there may be a chance you will date a non-Greek Orthodox Christian?

• Do you think you might intermarry one day?

• Is it important to consider your religious and cultural differences during the dating process?

• When should your religious and cultural differences be considered during the dating process?

• Why should you consider your religious and cultural differences during the dating process?

• What are some challenges that Greek Orthodox dating partners typically face?

• What are some challenges that the non-Greek Orthodox partner typically faces?

• Do you know the Orthodox Church's position regarding inter-Christian marriages?

• Do you know the Orthodox Church's position regarding interreligious marriages?

Chapter Nine

Challenges Engaged Couples Encounter

> "I hardly ever look back to the first few months after we got engaged because it's so painful. I had been dating John [a non-Greek Orthodox] for a about a year. My parents weren't thrilled, but they tolerated the situation. When I told them he proposed to me and I accepted, I expected them to be a little upset, but I wasn't prepared for their harsh reactions. For the next few months they threatened me, bribed me and were cold and nasty toward John. It was a very unsettling time. It got so bad that at one point we even thought about either eloping or calling the whole thing of. Then we went to see Father George. He helped us get through this rocky period and we are forever indebted to him."
>
> Focus Group Participant

The engagement period can be a very stressful time. After couples decide to get married, they suddenly encounter a number of challenges. Addressing individual needs, extended family concerns, coordinating guest lists, caterers, photographers, the florist, together with finding dates and times that suit the Church, their wedding party and reception hall are only a few of the tasks that couples must be concerned with. While most couples survive this process, modern wedding preparations are often anything but stress free experiences. Add to this, two people who come from different religious, ethnic, and in some instances, racial backgrounds, and the challenges may not only seem daunting, but endless.

Results from the IRP suggest that many couples from different ethnic and religious backgrounds encounter a host of challenges after they get engaged. What follows is a listing of some of the primary challenges, together with guidelines that could prove helpful to pastors as they attempt to assist engaged couples from a mixed Christian and ethnic background.[50] As you review the materials that follow, please remember that a wealth of information related to this population of couples is available in the intermarried couple's resource. Recommending this resource to couples should prove helpful to both you and them during the engagement period and throughout the marital life cycle.

Typical Extended Family Challenges

A General Observation. Extended families that viewed intermarriage from a positive perspective tended to have a positive effect on the dating process, engagement, and marriage. Positive extended family support was also construed as having a beneficial effect on couples' relationships with their parents and on family togetherness.

Family Resistance. Many participants' comments inferred that their parents' approval and happiness with their dating partner was important to them. While participants generally tried to find a partner who would please their parents and extended families, sometimes they were not successful. In these instances, participants described being caught between their desire to please their parents and their love and affection for their partner.

Most couples reported that parental disapproval disappeared as their relationship deepened. This seemed to be the case because parents did not wish to alienate their adult child. In most instances, initial resistance and disapproval would eventually disappear. In the place of parental resistance and disapproval, support would eventually emerge and new familial ties would begin forming.

A few participants reported that ill feelings lingered into the engagement period and through the first few years of marriage. Some also reported temporary and extended family cutoffs that occurred because of continued extended family displeasure. The following observations illustrate this. "We tried to be respectful to my parents after we got engaged, but there was no way of reasoning with them They simply didn't like Greg because he wasn't Greek. After a particularly distressing telephone conversation, I finally decided to let them know that I was in love with Greg and that we would be getting married with or without their blessings. Since that conversation, my father hasn't spoken to me and my mother has only recently – nearly a year after our marriage – begun to call. I've been deeply hurt, and it's been really hard to forgive them – especially my father who to this day doesn't appear to have softened one bit. The longer things linger, the more our lives drift apart and I become more convinced that I can live without them – although this saddens me deeply."

Couples' comments indicated that the length of time that their parents had spent in this country seemed to influence their reaction after they announced their engagement. Immigrant families and extended families that had only been in this country for one or two generations were more likely to have stronger ties to the mother country and thus offered more resistance to engaged couples. In relation to this point, because most Greek Orthodox extended families are relative newcomers to this country when compared to their non-Greek extended family counterparts, couples experiencing extended family resistance were generally referring to the Greek Orthodox partner's extended family. Many Greek Orthodox parents were described as valuing and encouraging single church and single culture marriages. "My parents are from Greece," stated one respondent, "so their initial disapproval was predictable. My wife's parents have been in this country almost since the pilgrims arrived, so they didn't care so long as she was marrying someone who was Christian."

In addition to parental pressure, pressure from Greek Orthodox grandparents was also repeatedly mentioned. In the words of one respondent, "Sure it's true that my parents gave me some grief over dating a non-Greek, but don't forget about *Yiayia* pressure. This kind of pressure can be even more pronounced than parental pressure." Big brother pressure was also another prominent type of pressure alluded to by some respondents. "Since my father died a few years ago, my brother has sort of looked after me and assumed his role. So, when he found out that I was thinking about marrying a non-Greek, he started acting like my father. It was at that point that I had to remind him I loved him, but he was my brother and I needed to make my own decisions about marriage. This didn't please him, but we eventually reached an understanding."

Conversely, families that had been in this country for a longer period of time were generally described as being less resistant to the notion of their son or daughter dating someone from a different ethnic and Christian background. Both the level of an extended family's ethnicity and the length of time that each spouse's family of origin had been in this country were directly associated with the amount of resistance and discouragement dating couples from different cultural and religious backgrounds encountered.

Some participants whose parents were both "very religious" and from Greece seemed to offer less resistance to their adult children. One respondent stated, "My parents, who are immigrants, never forced me to marry someone Greek. Certainly, they would not have objected to my marrying a Greek — I believe they would have preferred this — but they were more interested in whether he was Christian and had a good Christian heart. They are very religious people and it was more important to them that my husband be Christian rather than Greek."

Non-Greek Orthodox Reactions. When Greek Orthodox family members exerted pressure on their adult child to cool their involvement with their non-Orthodox dating partner, this tended to both confuse and insult some non-Orthodox who had been raised in families who had a nominal ethnic identity. Several non-Orthodox stated that they were not only confused by these attitudes toward non-Greeks, but also interpreted such attitudes as insulting and myopic in character.

Some non-Orthodox extended families were also generally described as valuing inter-Christian marriage as opposed to single-faith and single cultural marriage, and desired that their adult child marry a Christian rather than someone from the same ethnic and faith tradition. One possible exception to this was non-Orthodox extended families belonging to religious groups that have a fundamentalist, exclusive view of religion. In these instances, couples received high amounts of pressure from one or both parents belonging to these types of non-Orthodox religious groups. "My Mom is a strong believer," stated one non-Orthodox participant. "She belongs to a church that has some very conservative views. I mean, they believe that if you're not part of their church, you're not going to heaven. So, when she heard that I was considering marriage to a Greek Orthodox Christian she made things pretty difficult for us because she didn't hide her beliefs and disapproval. It's a little better now, but there's still a lot of tension in the air if the subject of religion comes up." Another possible exception was when the non-Orthodox extended family was new to this country. In these cases, such families mirrored Greek Orthodox extended family reactions.

If a couple chose to attend the Greek Orthodox Church on a regular basis, numerous participants observed that the religious and ethnic exclusivity frequently served to create tension between them and the non-Orthodox partner's extended family. Participants noted that non-Orthodox extended family members described feeling especially disconcerted with the Orthodox Church's rules regarding their participation in the sacraments. "My in-laws are still confused about the Orthodox Church's rules, and how they excluded them during our wedding and the baptism of our two children," stated one respondent. "And I don't think their attitude will change anytime soon." Several participants described hurt feelings that non-Orthodox extended family members felt when they were informed they could not function as a sponsor during the wedding or as a godparent. While the strategy was not always effective in addressing hurt feelings, it seems that when the Orthodox partner could respectfully articulate the Orthodox Church's position regarding non-Orthodox participation, hurt feelings were lessened. When the Orthodox partner was unable to offer a clear justification for the Orthodox Church's position, the hurt feelings were exacerbated. "I really think if I knew my faith better, some of the hard feelings that developed when we were selecting a godparent would not have occurred. I just didn't know how to tell my brother-in-law he couldn't assume this role without sounding really crass. If I knew what I know now, I think I could have deflected many of the misunderstandings that developed."

Pressures to wed in the Greek Orthodox Church

The Orthodox Church's pastoral guidelines can create challenges for couples. "The Orthodox Church has certain rules about where an Orthodox Christian can get married," stated one participant. "If I were to get married outside of the Orthodox Church, I would no longer be in good standing. So to satisfy this requirement, we decided to marry in the Orthodox Church. Besides, it was really no big sacrifice. We both loved the service, and so did everyone who attended."

Greek Orthodox parents can also exert a great deal of pressure on couples when they are deciding on where the wedding will take place. Some parents will make it known that they will offer their blessings as long as the couple agrees to marry in the Orthodox Church. As a result of the Orthodox Church's rules, together with Greek Orthodox parent's pressure, couples will generally determine to marry in the Orthodox Church. However, as you are well aware, getting to this point is not always easy. Sometimes couples encounter challenges.

Participants' comments suggested that some Greek Orthodox grandparents and parents tended to utilize excessive amounts of guilt and manipulation to convince the couples to get married and attend the Greek Orthodox Church after marriage. For example, in talking about his grandmother one respondent stated, "She started appealing to my conscience saying things like, 'this was your grandfather's church, how can you think about going anywhere else,' and 'what would he say if he were alive today.' Well, I knew what he would say, he would say that I needed to get married in my family's Church, and that made me feel real bad." These pressures tended to make the Greek Orthodox partner feel uncomfortable because, as one participant stated, "I began to feel as if I was caught between a rock and a hard place. It wasn't easy trying to please my family and my fiancée."

Additionally, if the Orthodox dating partner buckles under extended family pressure, and tries to convince his or her non-Orthodox spouse to get married in the Greek Orthodox Church, the non-Orthodox fiancée may feel both hurt and betrayed if he or she realizes what is happening. "He actually talked to his mother about our marriage taking place in the Greek Church before he talked to me. And that really hurt. I felt like, hey, this is my marriage, not hers. What business is it of hers until we've discussed it." In addition, Greek Orthodox spouses generally reported feeling guilty about siding with their family, and then angry at their family for introducing strife into the premarital process. While responding to this statement, the husband said, "Yes, she was right. I should have talked to her first. I was dead wrong…. and later I thought about how my mother kind of cornered me into this discussion and I was kind of angry with her. But it taught me an important lesson – never discuss things with your parents before you've discussed them with your spouse."

Finding ways of meeting the couple's needs, while also meeting extended family needs, is not easy for most couples, but it is possible. Generally, time, prayer, and honest respectful conversation can help, as can a discussion with the priest.

Pressure Lessens Before Marriage

Once it seemed apparent that a couple had decided to get married and nothing would change their minds, almost all extended families appeared to soften, and were considerably more supportive. This was especially true if a couple consented to worship in the Greek Orthodox Church. "It was just a matter of telling them," stated one respondent, "that we would be praying in the Greek Church, and that dissolved the tension and pressure among all of us."

This does not suggest that extended family challenges end at this point because many extended families require more time to warm up to someone from another religious and cultural/ ethnic background. Consider the following quote from one participant. "Don't misunderstand, my family really loves my husband, but it wasn't always like this. For some time after the marriage, things were somewhat unsteady between him and my family. But things are better now that we all figured out some stuff, and arrived at an understanding.... he became so much a part of us, that sometimes I think he's closer to my parents than I am."

Time, respect and an open-minded attitude on the part of all concerned are important as couples and extended families seek to coalesce and make the needed adjustments before the marriage takes place. If an engaged couple is experiencing family pressure before they wed, they should try to remember that most of these pressures will lift as they seek to meet their needs and the extended families' needs before the Sacrament of Marriage is celebrated.

Guidelines to Assist Clergy and Lay Workers

Personal, Couple and Family Challenges. Information from the IRP indicates that engaged couples from different faith groups and ethnic traditions desiring to wed in the Greek Orthodox Church will be confronted with many unique individual, couple and family challenges. While most of these couples will generally not approach you for counsel as they seek to resolve their challenges, at minimum, your sensitivity for their unique needs and challenges will facilitate trust and make the premarital preparation process less stressful.

Should a couple approach you requesting your feedback and counsel regarding certain individual, couple or family challenges they may be experiencing during the premarital process, you can be a valuable resource. Your pastoral experience and faithful, prayerful example can help facilitate conflict resolution. Working with the couple can be a positive opportunity to present the church as welcoming and compassionate. However, when it comes to dealing with individual, couple and family issues that appear to be of extreme nature and, or beyond your expertise, you are strongly advised to remember your limitations and refer out.[51] Providing the couple names of one or two trusted professionals may be a good choice in these instances.[52] This does not suggest that you have to relinquish responsibility for the issues in question when you refer out. With the couples' permission, psychotherapists are generally very receptive to collaborating with clergy in an effort to help their clients resolve presenting problems. If you find that he or she is not receptive to collaboration, you should continue looking for a better referral.

Depending on the situation, when referring out, try to anticipate any concerns. In most instances, the couple may not show it, but they will be wondering why you are offering this referral. They may also become inappropriately concerned. That is because there is still a stigma attached to those who seek help from a mental health professional. Softening their concerns with counsel such as the following will help: "I realize you might be wondering why I am referring you to Dr. "X." I know his (or her) work and trust that a few visits might be beneficial.

I will continue to provide you with religious and spiritual support, but I feel she (or he) can complement what we are doing. While I certainly will not force you to consider this option, I hope you will prayerfully consider this as an opportunity to grow closer to one another and enhance future martial satisfaction. Should you choose to follow up on this suggestion, I do not feel you will regret it." Letting them know they may benefit from another professional's observations because you feel as if you are exceeding your expertise is the responsible thing to do. Such an initiative also sends a message to the couple that the church seeks to promote healthy, holy unions in Christ. Some examples – but certainly not all examples – that might warrant a referral are as follows:

• When you detect physical or verbal abuse.

• When the couple's core belief system radically conflicts regarding (a) money, (b) parenting, (c) in-laws and (d) sex.

• When the couple seems to lack conflict resolution skills.

• When you suspect that one or both partners may be dealing with a form of mental illness such as clinical depression or some anxiety disorder.

During Your First Meeting. Most couples requesting the Sacrament of Marriage are not window shopping. They have discussed this issue extensively and are genuinely interested in getting married in the Greek Orthodox Church. They will also be nervous and be wondering what new challenges and obstacles they will encounter. Letting them know that you are interested in helping them is a good way to begin. Another sound approach will be to spend some time getting to know them better – especially the non-Orthodox partner. Information from the IRP suggests that first impressions went a long way in helping the non-Orthodox partner discern if the Greek Orthodox Church may be amenable to strangers.

After exchanging a few amenities and getting to know them better, at some point you will need to remind them that you are interested in helping them meet their needs but are also entrusted with following the Orthodox Church's pastoral guidelines. Let them also know that you will try and meet their needs so long as their requests do not conflict with either the Orthodox Church's pastoral guidelines or your Hierarch's directives. In most instances, this approach should suffice in helping you develop a good working relationship during the beginning of the premarital process.

Should the couple fail to ask any questions during this first meeting, do not assume they have no additional questions. Most will be reluctant to ask questions until they reach a certain level of comfort. As such, be sure to provide ample time and room for questions. You might also consider introducing questions into the process that other couples have asked you. (*Warning:* As many of you already know, there is nothing worse than receiving a complaint the next day from a parent or one or both partners accusing you of being insensitive and overly dogmatic. So, try and generate a respectful atmosphere that welcomes questions and concerns. Being proactive in this way will help cultivate trust and rapport between you and the couple.)

To avoid conflict and misunderstandings, once you have established some trust, you should carefully review the Orthodox Church's pastoral directives with all couples, and provide ample opportunity for individual concerns and questions. By taking this proactive approach you will be sending a message to the couple that you are interested in helping them get married in the Greek Orthodox Church in a responsible manner. (Please refer to Chapter 12 for a listing of pastoral directives pertaining to inter-Christian couples.)

Expect Difficult Questions. You might also remember that many of these couples may have received some misinformation regarding the Orthodox Church's pastoral guidelines prior to meeting with you. So, do not be terribly surprised or unsettled if they begin asking you to explain some of the Orthodox Church's pastoral guidelines as they pertain to intermarried couples. Please remember that most of their questions will generally be related to their lack of knowledge and their desire to respect the Orthodox Church's rules.

Please also remember that these couples will be seeking to reconcile pastoral guidelines from two different religious traditions in order to meet individual, couple and extended family needs. In consequence, they may be anxious, and some of their questions may sound disrespectful and abrasive. For example, some typical questions follow:

Why can't non-Orthodox clergy participate in the sacrament?

Why can't members of the non-Orthodox partner's family function as the *Paranymphos* or *Paranymphy*?

What is the Orthodox Church's interpretation of Ephesians 5: 21-33?

In your attempts to address their questions and concerns, remember that many of these couples espouse an ecumenical perspective of the church. This means that they will generally conceptualize Christianity as being made up of many segments or denominations. There are many reasons to explain why this is the case. However, knowing the reasons are not as relevant here as being aware that this will typically be true of some of these couples. Furthermore, this knowledge should help you avoid some pitfalls that could compromise your effectiveness. For example, getting into theological debates around this issue will likely do little to enhance trust and convince the couple that marriage in the Greek Orthodox Church is the correct choice for them. Such exchanges will likely also undermine the non-Orthodox partner's perception of the Orthodox Church. All this is not to suggest that you refrain from explicating the Orthodox Church's position, since most couples will generally be satisfied when you respectfully offer sound Orthodox theological reasons to justify the Orthodox Church's theology and pastoral guidelines in a non-combative manner.

Being intimately familiar with Orthodox ecclesiology, sacramental theology, canonical tradition and the GOA's pastoral guidelines as they pertain to couples from an inter-Christian background is also essential.[53] So, do not hesitate to offer information about the Orthodox Church, but take some care in entering into debates with strong-willed people. An old adage may be useful to keep in mind here: *You could win the battle, but lose the war*. In other words, you will likely be able to win the debate, but the residual effects of this victory could compromise this couple's long-term relationship with the Orthodox Church. Respectful conversation that avoids debate, and seeks to speak the truth in love will best serve this process.

Should you continue receiving objections, a good course of action might be to politely evaluate the couple's motives and reasons for wanting to get married in the Greek Orthodox Church. As you allow them to tell their story, it is likely that you will discover that one or both spouses may begrudgingly have agreed to wed in the Orthodox Church because of extended family pressure, and, or pressure from the Greek Orthodox partner. In these cases you might consider spending more time helping such couples come to some mutually satisfying resolutions before proceeding with the premarital process. Before doing this work, politely let the couple know that research clearly indicates that unresolved issues can fester and undermine future marital satisfaction and family stability. Resolution of these issues can help them develop needed couple's skills and ensure that the first stage in the marital life cycle is free of serious differences.[54]

Asking couples the following question and then listening patiently may help both you and them discern some of the sources of discontent: *Why have you chosen to get married in the Orthodox Church?* If done with care and respect, a conversation could unfold that can help couples determine if marriage in the Orthodox Church is an appropriate choice for them at this time. Couples who are unable to work through this question are likely good candidates for a referral to a professional.

The Pros and Cons of Intermarriage. In your efforts to be respectful, it is not inappropriate to ask if the couple has considered the pros and cons of becoming a single-church couple.[55] Most couples will appreciate this initiative if it is done respectfully. However, some may experience some anxiety – especially the non-Orthodox partner. Prefacing your remarks with statements like those that follow will serve to reduce their concern and anxiety. "What I am about to say in no way questions your decision to intermarry. In offering this information, I only have your future well-being in mind. What you decide to do with this information is up to the non-Orthodox partner, the two of you and God. If what I say evokes some anxiety, concerns or questions, I would be happy to help you address them." You might then offer them the following information, and also recommend that they review the materials in the intermarried couple's resource.

• Many engaged couples fail to deal with the issue I am about to introduce, because they figure it is "no big deal." In some instances, that is correct, but in other instances it is far from being accurate.

• Social science has taught us that people's core values are influenced by religion and culture. We also know that the lens that people use to view the world is highly influenced by their religious and cultural backgrounds. [56] So, even though it may not seem to be the case today, religion and culture are more important than most young couples assume. As people age, research clearly indicates that they become more religious and closer to their cultural roots.[57]

• While many intermarried couples report being happily married, research indicates that the more differences that couples have the more challenges they will experience. This may be one reason why the divorce rate among intramarried[58] couples is lower when compared to intermarried couples. (If the couple desires more specific information regarding the additional challenges that intermarried couples face, refer them to the intermarried couple's resource.)

• Statistics also suggest that intermarried couples encounter more parental challenges related to their children's religious and spiritual development. Moreover, these increased challenges can often have a negative impact on children's religious development. (If the couple desires more information, refer them to the intermarried couple's resource.)

• I have offered this information to help you understand the challenges of intermarriage and would like to bring up several options. Please understand that it is not my intent to force or manipulate you into doing anything you do not want to do, but am only presenting you with options.

• You can get married in the Orthodox Church and remain an intermarried couple. Many people have done this successfully. Descriptions from the intermarried couples resource clearly support this observation. Moreover, the Orthodox Church welcomes everyone to its family. However, you should also keep in mind that the non-Orthodox partner cannot partake of the sacraments.

• You can also consider becoming a single-church couple. In short, if there are no extenuating circumstances that preclude you from prayerfully considering this option, I encourage you to do so. That is because the more things that couples have in common, the more likelihood they will encounter higher levels of future marital satisfaction. (If the couple seems interested, ask the non-Orthodox partner if he or she would like more information.)

You should also be careful not to ask too many more questions or appear too eager to get the couple to consider this issue. Too much enthusiasm and too many uninvited questions may seem pushy and intrusive. Simply reiterate that your intentions are to help them, and you do not presume to know what is good for them. Then suggest that they should consider this option prayerfully and that you will be asking them what they have decided at your next meeting. (Please remember to refer them to the last chapter of the intermarried couples' resource – especially the questionnaire that assesses their readiness to intermarry.)

In the end, being aware of the unique challenges that engaged couples encounter will facilitate your effectiveness during the premarital preparation process. Your increased knowledge of this population's idiosyncrasies should also help you cultivate a closer relationship with these couples. This will prove beneficial to them as they struggle to become a part of the faithful who worship in the Greek Orthodox Church you serve.

An Exercise for the GOYA and YAL

Young people in the community you serve will likely have never been exposed to the above materials. Finding ways of making some of this knowledge available to them early should serve them well in the near future when they are considering engagement and marriage.

Pastors and other church workers should think about presenting some of the information in this chapter. There are many ways to accomplish this. Below you will find some key questions that should become part of this effort. (The more creative you are in presenting some of these questions and the underlying challenges they contain, the greater the positive impact they will have on your teens and young adults.)

• Did you know that over 70% of Greek Orthodox young adults intermarry?

• Do you think there is a chance you might intermarry one day?

• On a scale of 1-10, with one representing "not at all," and ten representing "absolutely central to who I am and how I think," how important is your Greek Orthodox background to you?

• Even if your religious and cultural background isn't real important to you, did you know that religion and culture become more important to people as they mature?

• Is it important to consider your religious and cultural differences during the engagement period?

• After you get engaged, when should your religious and cultural differences be discussed?

• Why do you think couples fail to discuss their religious and cultural differences?

• Did you know that engaged partners who have equally strong connections to their religious backgrounds will encounter the most challenges during the engagement period?

• Why do you think this is the case?

• Did you know that in cases where one partner has a high level of religious connection and the other has a low level of religious connection, this difference can potentially create future marital problems?

• What kinds of challenges do engaged couples encounter from their extended families?

• What are some challenges that Greek Orthodox engaged partners typically face?

• What are some challenges that the non-Greek Orthodox partner typically faces?

• Do you know the Orthodox Church's position regarding inter-Christian marriages?

• Do you know the Orthodox Church's position regarding interreligious marriages?

Chapter Ten

CHALLENGES NEWLYWEDS FACE AFTER MARRIAGE

> "When we got married, I never imagined how much my religious, and to lesser extent, ethnic background mattered. Bob's parents – especially his mother – really wanted us to attend her church. She was also privately critical of my Greek Orthodox heritage. These private discussions started creating some real challenges between us about six months into our marriage. With Father Peter's help and the help of a good marital counselor, we were able to learn how to prevent his parents' unwanted opinions and advice from doing any serious damage to our marriage."
>
> Focus Group Participant

After the honeymoon is over, couples enter an adjustment period. The old adage that there are six people in the marriage bed rather than two is correct. That is because we bring with us certain expectations about marriage that we learned from our parents. One primary challenge facing all newlyweds is to take two different backgrounds and meld them into a common existence. In relation to this challenge, issues related to money, sex, communication, recreation, careers, friends, housework and in-laws surface. Generally speaking, intermarried couples' religious and cultural differences further complicate this adjustment period. The following information from the IRP serves to illustrate this point.

A General Observation. According to the IRP, most intermarried couples are able to successfully negotiate challenges related to their religious and cultural differences. However, some experience moderate to serious difficulty that compromises marital satisfaction. Those participants who believed that their religious and cultural differences enriched their lives were less inclined to experience long-term negative effects. They reported higher levels of religious commitment and church attendance. Intermarried couples who experienced lingering difficulties tended to view those differences as threats to marital and family stability and satisfaction. They were less likely to be active, supportive church members during this stage in the life cycle.

Culture Shock.[59] While both partners may experience some degree of culture shock, results from the IRP suggest that the non-Orthodox partner is prone to experience more discomfort when introduced to their spouses' Greek Orthodox background. In most cases, insecurity and unfamiliarity with their partner's cultural and religious idiosyncrasies tended to be resolved with time. Spouses who continued to report uneasiness reported low levels of marital satisfaction.

Deciding Where to Pray. Most couples reported that their religious needs did not present them with serious challenges during this stage. Many indicated that they simply alternated churches. Others chose to attend the more religious partner's church. Exceptions were when both partners were highly committed to their religious tradition. Those with high interest reported some moderate to serious disagreements in their efforts to meet their religious needs both as individuals and as couples. In these cases, both spouses generally attended their own churches. While this accommodation seemed to meet their individual religious needs, it often fell short of meeting their religious needs as a couple.

In-Laws and Extended Family. Most couples described an awkward adjustment period between themselves and their in-laws. Generally this period did not last long. However, in some instances, intergenerational relations remained distant for years.

The non-Greek Orthodox partner seemed to experience more of these types of challenges than the Greek Orthodox spouse.[60] This seemed to be the case when lingering issues during the engagement period remained unresolved. In these particular cases, observations from the IRP consistently identified two patterns. When the Greek Orthodox partner's extended family failed to accept the marriage, they either blamed the non-Orthodox partner or blamed both spouses. Cutoffs between the couple and extended family members were not unusual in these instances.

Results from the IRP also indicated that it was important for newlyweds to draw healthy boundaries between themselves and their parents. Keeping out unwanted extended family intrusions was important to couples' efforts to mold and shape a life together. Finding ways to honor their parents while also making their own decisions was of critical importance to newly intermarried couples.

Praying Together. Most of these couples indicated that their faith in God was indispensable in their efforts to strike a balance between personal, couple, and extended family needs. Given their religious differences, some couples were challenged to find ways to pray together. Because of their common Christian backgrounds, most couples succeeded. Those who struggled to develop a prayer life together found that in doing so, stresses and strains of developing a life together were minimized.

Guidelines That Might Assist Clergy and Lay Leaders

Individual and Couple Challenges. Most newlyweds will adjust to married life without outside help. However, some couples will confront serious problems that they will be unable to negotiate alone.[61] Some of these problems may be related to their religious and cultural differences.[62] When this occurs, they may approach you. When they do, the above information, together with the guidelines that follow should prove helpful.

Results from the IRP indicate that if a couple is experiencing problems related specifically to their religious and cultural differences, the Greek Orthodox partner will most likely be the one to approach you seeking help. In a few instances, the non-Orthodox partner might be the first to request your help, while in other instances the couple or the couple's parents may approach you. No matter who comes to you, the important thing to remember here is that a request for help is being made[63].

When this occurs, please remember that you have some valuable skills that can make a difference. All too often priests underestimate their expertise and determine to refer out. The opposite reaction can also occur, when clergy misjudge their abilities and quickly find themselves over their heads. So, respect your skills and their limitations. If you are approached for help, here is some information for your consideration.

The first thing you should do is listen carefully to the individual's or couple's story before offering any advice or suggestions. The more information you obtain, the higher the probability your counsel will relate to their challenges. An example of what *not* to do follows.

Sophia approaches Father Nick on Sunday during the coffee hour for some strategies that could help her convince her spouse to attend Divine Liturgy. Father Nick is overcommitted with numerous concerns and does not have time to listen carefully. He offers the following suggestions that have worked for other couples in the past. "Just tell him you're tired of attending church alone and you want him to start coming with you. Stay committed to this approach, and ask God to help you. Trust me, he'll come around. I've seen this work for others." Sophia departs encouraged and eager to test this new strategy. On the following Sunday while the couple is preparing to go to church, she offers the following ultimatum to her spouse. "I've been thinking about this for a few months. I'm tired of going to church alone. I want you to start coming with me. I spoke with Father Nick, and he agrees this is a good idea." When her spouse hears this, he is offended and a disagreement ensues. The couple fails to attend church that morning, nothing is resolved, and for the next several months there is tension between them over this issue – especially on Sunday mornings. Fortunately, the couple is eventually able to make some adjustments which takes into account both partner's religious needs. However, it takes them much longer to feel comfortable about approaching Father Nick for guidance.

Why was Father Nick's counsel ineffective? The answer is simple. As a result of being preoccupied, he offered counsel – however well intended – without knowing all the facts. For example, Father Nick was not aware that Sophia had been getting a great deal of pressure from her grandmother to get her spouse to Divine Liturgy, and this promoted her to seek pastoral counsel. He was also not aware that Sophia's husband had a high religious commitment to his own church. A more effective response would have been to suggest that Sophia make an appointment. During a private conversation Father Nick would then have ample time to begin developing a better understanding of Sophia's challenge before offering any observations. Remember that what might have worked for one couple may not always work well for another couple because of the disparate family issues in which a given challenge is embedded.

You might also remember that when individuals approach you, they may be less interested in your counsel and more interested in strengthening and justifying their own personal position. Exploring this possibility before offering any feedback and direction is also another good policy. Your best chance to help these couples is to retain a neutral position that provides counsel and facilitates prayerful change. Being perceived as biased by one partner – usually the non-Orthodox partner – can compromise your relationship with this couple. This perception can strongly affect the couple's decision to worship in the Greek Orthodox Church.[64]

When offering counsel, remind the individual or couple that they must work together toward resolving this issue. A unilateral strategy that ignores either partner's needs and concerns will only serve to undermine marital satisfaction. This is particularly relevant to newlyweds who are in the process of developing conflict resolution skills. Listening carefully and being patient while holding to a neutral position that considers both partners' needs is a good pastoral approach.

At some juncture during your first meeting, make certain to respectfully inform one or both partners of the Orthodox Church's position regarding their current challenge. This information will empower them to reach a mutually satisfying resolution. Such an approach will also engender respect into the process for the Orthodox Church's pastoral guidelines. The following example illustrates these observations.

Sam presented Father Joseph with the following problem, "My wife refuses to come to church with me because she feels it's only for Greeks. I've told her she's wrong, and that she is welcome. I've also told her that receiving communion together would bring us closer to one another." With regard to Sam's second comment, Father Joseph is reluctant to offer him feedback regarding the Orthodox Church's position on intercommunion at that moment. He wants to hear more of his story, but also fears that Sam may become more discouraged if he were offered the Orthodox Church's position on intercommunion. Instead, he decides to withhold this information until a more opportune time. The problem is, a better time never presents itself and his reticence only makes matters worse because this issue is never broached.

Toward the end of their second meeting when Sam is finally informed about the Orthodox Church's position regarding sacramental participation, Sam becomes visibly agitated and very discouraged. Out of frustration, he says, "I really wish you had told me this during our first meeting. Now I have to go back and inform my wife that she can't receive the sacraments. This will simply reinforce what she's already believes about the Greek Orthodox Church – that it's only for Greeks." No matter how much Father Joseph tries to explain why this happens, Sam is focused on two things – his wife's reactions to this news and Father Joseph's failure to provide timely information.

Relevant and timely information might have facilitated Sam's efforts. As it was, Father Joseph's delayed response exacerbated this couple's efforts to reach a mutually satisfying decision. To that end, do not assume that intermarried couples know the Orthodox Church's position on a given topic. Information from the IRP suggests that most couples are confused and unaware of the Orthodox Church's rules, worship and practices. So, always take the time to educate intermarried couples in a respectful way with regard to the Church's pastoral guidelines. This is a good rule of thumb to follow even if you discern the individual or couple is familiar with the Orthodox Church's position. In most cases you will deepen their understanding of a subject they assumed they understood. In addition, it is a good habit to respectfully offer this information as soon as possible. Such an approach will provide them with the information they need in order to resolve any challenges related to their religious differences. These teaching moments will also engender respect for the Orthodox Church's perspective.

Incidentally, pastoral situations like the ones described in this chapter are excellent teaching opportunities to promote marriage from an Orthodox/Christian perspective. In addition to helping couples resolve their intermarried challenges, please remember to take the time to help them understand the difference between a Christian/Orthodox marriage and the postmodern, secular models of marriage that our society promotes. Talk to one or both spouses about the self-sacrificial nature of marriage. Emphasize themes like commitment, forgiveness, prayer and God's grace, and remind them that the present struggle they have described affords them an opportunity to grow closer to each other and God.

In some cases, you will also encounter individuals requesting a "how to" approach. If this occurs, unless they are willing to collaborate with you in creating a strategy to resolve their issues, you should avoid the temptation to provide a specific plan. Assuming a neutral, not knowing, curious role will encourage the couple or spouse to take a proactive approach in their efforts to resolve their challenges.[65] Offering specific advice without the couple's input is generally a recipe for failure that could come back to haunt you. In most instances, avoid offering specific advice and concentrate on providing information, suggestions and observations that one or both partners can utilize in their efforts to resolve their present challenge.

If the person or couple insists upon obtaining concrete direction, you might consider prefacing any counsel with the following comments: "While I don't think it's generally wise to tell people what they should do, since you appear to need some direction, if I were faced with your challenge(s) I might…."

Making a follow-up phone call in a few days may also prove to be a wise choice in these instances. A phone call after your meeting will not only allow you to remain in contact with the individual or couple, but it may also positively impact their future participation, support and commitment.

You might also remember that most of these issues are related to the couple's failure to either discuss or reach closure regarding their religious and cultural differences before marriage. As such, reminding them that adjustments are typical after marriage and that a prayerful solution will emerge should help normalize their challenge and reduce their anxiety.

Additionally, many newlyweds who approach you may be encountering their first serious disagreement. Such couples or individuals might be wondering if their present problems are signaling the beginning of the end of their marriage. Reminding them that disagreements are part of being married might be of great value. They will also be comforted if you remind them that God's grace and their faith in God will assist them in finding a resolution to their present unsettling challenge. Consider the following example.

Maria approached Father Chris visibly distraught. She indicates that she and her husband had their first serious disagreement. She also is wondering about the future well-being of her new marriage. After listening to Maria, Father Chris discovers that the couple is at odds with one another regarding church attendance. Her husband wants the couple to attend his church periodically and she is disinterested in this suggestion. The end result is that her husband has refused to come to the Greek Orthodox Church for several weeks and they are generally not talking with each other. In consequence, Father Chris advises her not to be too concerned over what has happened, because all couple's argue, and arguments can be healthy so long as they lead to some mutually satisfying resolutions. He also cautions her to try and break this stalemate by asking her husbands forgiveness. He reminds her that lingering disagreements are contrary to God's will, because they are divisive to the couple's individual and marital religious and spiritual well-being. He further encourages her to continue discussing this issue respectfully, while making certain that she is aware that he is available should she or the couple desire to speak to him.

Extended Family Challenges. In some cases, a spouse or couple may approach you regarding an extended family issue. If this occurs, the following general protocol should prove helpful.

Listen carefully to their story and avoid making comments until you have a good understanding of the problem. Additionally, your understanding of the problem should include all involved parties needs and concerns. For instance, are both partners' extended families involved? Which members of the extended family seem like key players in this disagreement? Additionally, try to avoid assuming complete responsibility for this problem. Make the individual or couple aware that you will be happy to provide some pastoral direction, but they will be entrusted with working through their present challenge with God's help and your support. According to the results from the IRP, most couples will appreciate this approach.

In some cases, you may feel overwhelmed after you have heard their story. If this occurs, you may want to consider offering a referral with the understanding that you will continue to provide religious and spiritual counsel. It is better to admit your limitations upfront rather than after several failed attempts at offering suggestions. Information from the IRP suggests that most couples will respect and appreciate your honesty.

You might also remind the couple that it is not unusual for newlyweds to experience extended family challenges. Tell them that it may seem difficult to draw some healthy boundaries between themselves and their extended families, but this is normal and healthy. Spending some time with these couples discussing the Biblical injunction to honor father and mother should also prove helpful. In these conversations you might help them understand that they can honor and respect their parents without necessarily allowing their parents to intrude in their marital and future family decisions. The following example should help reinforce what has been written in this section.

Peter approaches Father Steve for some help. It appears that his mother and wife have locked horns regarding this year's Christmas dinner menu. His mother wants the menu to be exclusively Greek and his wife wants to offer a combination of Greek and non-Greek foods and pastries. Peter feels as if he is locked in a lose/lose situation and has been reluctant to side with either his wife or mother. This has promoted his mother to make some rather distasteful remarks in private to him about his wife. This disagreement has also caused his wife to feel as if Peter is siding with his mother.

Father Steve listens to him and offers the following observations. "It is not unusual for newlyweds to feel these mixed allegiances early on in marriage. So, please remember that you are trying to build a life with your wife. In some cases, parent's observations may prove helpful, but not when they serve to divide you and your wife. I would have a private conversation with your mother informing her that you love and respect her and that you and your wife will try and respect her suggestions. However, since the dinner is in your home, you and your wife will make the final decision regarding the foods and pastries that will be offered. I would also inform your wife of this conversation and ask her forgiveness."

Parents' Concerns. When parents approach you for help, you should remember that most are not expecting you to resolve their problems. Simply providing an attentive, supportive, comforting ear will be all most parents expect and require.

In these pastoral situations, remind parents that adjustments are typical between parents and newlyweds. You might also respectfully forewarn them to foster a respectful and supportive posture when it comes to the newlywed's issues and challenges. For example, remind them that unsolicited advice and intrusions will generally backfire and could actually exacerbate the couple's problems. Then respectfully tell them that the best help they could provide is to intercede only when spouse abuse[66] is suspected or if they suspect the couple is in need of some outside professional intervention.

While this may be rare, some parents may expect you to collude with them in their efforts to help their adult child and his or her marriage. In these instances, you will likely know these parents, so please remember that your own objectivity may be compromised by your relationship with them. The best assistance you can offer might be to refer them to an outside resource. Otherwise, you may find yourself succumbing to the temptation to sympathize and agree with the parents, irrespective of what is good for the couple.

Listening respectfully and carefully is a good first step. Offering some general prayerful counsel is a good second step. Additionally, counsel parents so that they afford their children ample space to work out their marital conflicts. Let parents also know that they should assume the role of advisor and only offer input when it is requested or when matters absolutely warrant outside intervention. You might also indicate that you would be happy to assist the couple if one or both spouses request your help. If the parents seem desperate and you discern additional pastoral care is warranted, you could be amenable to calling the couple to volunteer your help. The following example may help reinforce what has been written in this section.

Anastasia and Gus approach their priest for some help. Both suspect that their daughter and son-in-law are attending a local non-denominational church. They also believe that their son-in-law is forcing their daughter to attend this church. They want him to call the couple. The priest listens and sympathizes with this couple. He tells them that he would also feel like them if one of his children decided to worship outside of the Greek Orthodox Church. He also reminds them that too much pushing can only result in creating a serious family disagreement or cutoff. Since they still desire his help, he agrees to make a call, but does not promise anything.

When he calls, the daughter answers the phone. After a few amenities are shared, the priest indicates that he had not seen the couple in church since the wedding and was wondering how they were and if they needed anything. The daughter states that they are well and have simply been busy. He asks when he might see them, and she states that they would likely come to church in the near future. The priest then reminds her that he will anticipate their next visit and states that he might call again in the future. The daughter does not indicate any objections and the conversation ends.

In this case, the priest might have chosen to confront the daughter with all the facts, but this might have proven divisive. In challenging the daughter with the information he had, he might have caused a family rift and further compromised his relationship with the couple and alienated the daughter from the Orthodox Church. By leaving the door open for more contact this strategy served to respect the couple, meet the parents' needs and keep a connection between the couple and the Orthodox Church.

A Final Caveat. Whenever working with conflicted family systems, you must consider your experience and comfort level. This type of pastoral counseling can be very stressful and challenging. So, there is no crime in recognizing your limitations. If you are feeling overwhelmed, consult a brother priest for a second opinion. If you are still feeling overwhelmed, make your limitations known and offer the names of two or three professionals who specialize in working with conflicted families and couples.[67] You can continue to offer spiritual guidance and support while not being entirely responsible for the marital and family problems.

An Exercise for Single and Married Young Adults

The young adults in the community you serve (both married and single) are likely to have never been exposed to most of the challenges that intermarried newlyweds face. Finding ways of making some of this knowledge available to them early should serve them well in the near future. Pastors and other church workers should think about ways that they can present some of the information to them. Here are two suggestions. You might consider inviting a speaker to conduct a marriage building retreat. Since the cost of this approach may be high, such an event could be co-sponsored by several local churches. This retreat could feature a speaker who would introduce many of these concepts. Another way is to present this material to the YAL in a way that seeks to generate conversation. The following questions should help should you choose either suggestion.

Can you draw some differences between Christ-centered marriages and marriage according to the popular media?

How do marriages fail?

What are some strategies that help couples protect their marriage?

What are some personal challenges that intermarried newlyweds might face?

What are some challenges that couples might face?

What are some extended family challenges that intermarried couples might face?

What happens when personal needs and couple needs conflict?

What happens when the couple's challenges and extended family challenges conflict?

What are some balancing strategies that couples can employ to help them resolve these different types of challenges?

How can spouses' and couples' Christian faith help resolve these challenges?

Chapter Eleven

From Conception Through Young Adulthood: Challenges That Parents Encounter As Their Children Mature

> "We've been struggling with a number of issues related to our different religious backgrounds. So I was very happy to discover the information on the Interfaith Marriage Web site. Reviewing this information gave us some new insights and helped us understand that we are not alone. Somehow it was comforting knowing that our problems are not that much different than others who intermarry. Thanks again, and may God continue to bless this work."
>
> An E-mail Respondent

I have received and addressed hundreds of messages since beginning my work, many of which expressed sentiments similar to what the above respondent has written. In most cases, individuals were seeking information that would help them understand and resolve a particular challenge related to their different religious and ethnic backgrounds. However, a substantial percentage – perhaps 25% – described numerous challenges of a more serious nature that required some additional support and direction.

In light of what I have encountered, this chapter has been structured in a manner which reflects the pastoral needs I have discovered while working with hundreds of intermarried couples. In the first part of this chapter, you can expect to review information that pertains to the following stages in the family life cycle: (a) starting a family, (b) when the children begin maturing, (c) families with adolescents, (d) families with young adults, and (e) the empty nest. This section will also offer some suggestions to help you present these materials to intermarried couples in your parish. The last part of this chapter will continue describing key components of a pastoral approach that I have utilized when ministering to conflicted intermarried spouses, couples and their families. Should a troubled intermarried couple approach you for some help, this section will provide you with some guidelines to assist you in your efforts to help them find some mutually satisfying and holy resolutions.

Challenges Related to Starting a Family

> "We were sort of coasting – problem free – until we decided to have children. All of a sudden, it was like someone opened a can of worms and we started having all kinds of disagreements. Fortunately, we were able to find some help. Our priests were especially helpful."
>
> Focus Group Participant

Most couples decide to begin a family after a few years of marriage. When the first child arrives, couples are challenged to maintain a balance between work life and home life. Children's presence also deprives them of privacy and emotional and sexual intimacy. Extended family challenges also become more prominent since a couple's focus moves away from an emphasis on marriage and more toward past and future generational concerns. It is no wonder marital satisfaction tends to suffer during this time.[68] Along with the typical challenges that all couples face when newly married, intermarried couples can expect to encounter additional challenges. These are related to their religious and cultural differences. Here are some typical challenges that couples will face.

• If couples have failed to discuss where their children will be baptized, and in which church they will be raised before marriage, some conversation regarding these questions will likely occur around the time of the first child's arrival. Couples with equally strong attachments to their religious and ethnic backgrounds may have more difficulties negotiating these questions, than couples where one partner is more religious than the other. Couples with equally low levels of religious and ethnic attachments may not experience much conflict resolving these questions. However, these couples may experience other issues related to their different levels of religious commitment as the children mature.

• Finding ways to strike a balance between each spouse's desire to baptize the future children in his or her faith community, to do what is best for them, and their desire to respectfully consider their spouse's opinion, can create tension between couples. Unspoken assumptions before marriage regarding this issue can also trigger disappointment and hurt feelings that can lead to marital conflict. Such feelings and thoughts can potentially linger for years and undermine family members' religious and spiritual development.

• The grandparents' yearnings to see their children baptized and raised in their faith community can also present some challenges to intermarried couples. Grandparents may apply pressure on their adult children that can create even more tension between couples who have conflicted feelings over the issue of baptism. Unwanted grandparent intrusions and pressures can serve to convolute parents' efforts to resolve this issue, as well as compromise growing relationships with extended family members. Couples will be challenged to find respectful ways of drawing healthy boundaries between themselves and their extended families in their efforts to arrive at a mutually satisfying decision regarding their children's baptism. Concurrently, couples will be challenged to honor parents while drawing these boundaries.

• Some couples will also struggle with the Greek tradition that encourages Greek parents to name the first-born son after the Greek Orthodox spouse's father. The Greek Orthodox partner may feel a deep need to honor the parent in this way, while the non-Orthodox partner frequently views this tradition as a cultural intrusion. Finding ways of striking a balance between personal, couple, and extended family needs in this situation can generate marital, family and extended family tension. In some instances, couples will choose to give their children two names, a legal name and a baptismal name. In other cases, one or the other partner will make a concession. In the worst of cases, one partner will unilaterally make a decision regarding this issue that can potentially create lingering resentment in the other spouse.

• If the couple decides to baptize their children in the Greek Orthodox Church, the non-Orthodox partner and his or her extended family may feel somewhat short changed, especially since Orthodox pastoral guidelines prohibit non-Orthodox participation in the Sacraments. The Orthodox partner may feel varying degrees of resentment for these rules from the non-Orthodox spouse and his or her extended family. Finding ways of not personalizing this resentment will be helpful to nuclear and extended family stability and well-being.

• In order to meet the children's future religious and spiritual needs, many couples will eventually elect to attend the church where their children are baptized. When intermarried couples determine to baptize their child in the Greek Orthodox Church, and subsequently decide to attend the Orthodox Church, the non-Orthodox partner may struggle to avoid feeling like the odd-man-out when the family attends Divine Liturgy together. This is the case because non-Orthodox cannot participate in the Sacramental life of the Orthodox Church. Being aware of this potential pitfall can help both partners work through negative feelings and thoughts that might undermine family members' religious and spiritual development.

• Lingering hurt feelings related to the children's cultural development can be unhealthy for a couple's marriage and their children's development. For instance, the Greek Orthodox partner may want the children to learn Greek, while the other partner either undermines this effort or is indifferent to this need. Finding ways to address hurt feelings can be challenging since such discussions are viewed as potentially uncomfortable and counterproductive. Failure to ease hurt feelings could be detrimental to marital and family religious well-being.

When the Children Begin Maturing

> "For the first few years after the children arrived, we tried to go to both churches. But I soon realized that this plan wasn't workable. Around the time when our kids were about four, I insisted that we make up our minds and raise them in one church. Since I was the more religious one, we eventually chose my church. Since my husband decided to remain a Baptist Christian, we've never really gotten comfortable with this decision. But we do it for the kids."
>
> *Focus Group Participant*

As children mature, a couple's focus will shift from a preoccupation with their own relationship to a greater focus on their children's needs. Because of this, many couples who have previously been nominally interested in religion may show an increased interest in religious matters. This increased interest in religion can present inter-Christian couples with some challenges that single-church couples do not face. This section will describe some of these primary challenges. When couples become stuck and unable to resolve any one of these challenges, this failure generally has a negative effect on marital satisfaction and their children's religious development.

• Results from the IRP clearly indicate that intermarried couple's religious differences can potentially impede their children's efforts to develop a religious identity. The following comments illustrate this point. "Up until the last few years, we argued about the church we would attend. Tom's church didn't meet my needs, and my church didn't meet his.... The irony is that we were so caught-up in our own needs, that we forgot our children's needs. Now that our children have their own lives, all three have little interest in structured religion. I'm sure our arguments had something to do with this."

• When parents fail to provide their children with a consistent faith experience in one church, this can prevent them from developing a strong religious identity. Striking a balance between helping their children develop a keen respect for both parents' religious traditions, while also helping them bond to one faith tradition, can be a tricky proposition that intermarried parents may likely encounter. "We tried bringing them up in both churches," stated another respondent. "We thought that was the fairest solution. But we were dead wrong. All this approach did is prevent our children and family from ever finding a church home. I wouldn't recommend this to other intermarried parents."

• As children mature, they ask questions in an effort to piece their world together. As such, when children who live in an inter-Christian household observe their parents' different religious habits, they will naturally ask questions. Sometimes these questions can present real challenges. Typical questions may be: "Why doesn't Mom receive communion with us?" or, "Why doesn't Dad come to church with us?" or, "Why does Dad do his cross differently?" When parents are presented with these questions, they are not familiar enough with their own faith tradition or their partner's faith tradition to offer an adequate answer. Their natural tendency at these moments is to ignore the question(s) or tell the children "later." But this approach is just a way to buy some time. Most parents, for many reasons, never answer these questions, which means that children will either never have their questions answered or they will find their own answers. All too often, they may turn to their peers, other adult figures or the television for answers. Unless they are fortunate to find someone with a balanced perspective, they can begin developing a skewed perspective of religion. This of course will do little to facilitate religious and spiritual growth. As one father commented, "It wasn't until our oldest reached eight or nine when I started dreading the questions related to religion. Up until that time, I was sort of blowing the questions off half jokingly because I didn't know how to answer them. I also didn't want to disrespect my wife's religious background. One day while coming back from church our son said, 'Frank's

Mom said that religion is dumb because it makes problems between people. I kind of agree.' It's hard to describe the atmosphere in the car when he said this. But it wasn't good. We felt like we were losing part of our son. A few days later, we went to our priests and they recommended some age appropriate reading material. This new knowledge and proactive approach has made all the difference for us all."

• The parent who has agreed to baptize the children in the partner's faith tradition can also end up feeling somewhat distanced from the children in this area of their developing lives. This is especially the case when the parent has a moderate to strong religious attachment. One respondent described these feelings in this way. "I am Roman Catholic. So, I can't receive communion in the Greek Orthodox Church. Lately that's been really bothering me. It makes me feel empty because I can't participate in a very important part of my children's life. I know it sounds silly, but sometimes that hurts." Some of these parents might also feel some degree of loss as a result of their decision to baptize the children in the partner's church. "When the children first arrived, I agreed to baptize the children in the Greek Church. As they've gotten older, sometimes I resent the fact that I can't share what I experienced as a child with them because they belong to my husband's church."

• Spouses who have had their children baptized in their church can also end up feeling some guilt when they become aware of their partner's feelings. In these instances, ongoing discussion is necessary to ensure that these negative feelings do not impact couple and family well-being. "Hank is a very religious guy, and sometimes I feel sort of guilty for asking him to baptize the children in the Greek Church. I know he loves me and that's why he did it. But sometimes I've detected moments when he's been hurt about this and we needed to talk things out. I think these discussions have helped us both."

• Extended family pressures are generally of minimal concern at this point in the family life cycle. Couples have generally managed to develop healthy boundaries between themselves and their respective families. Nevertheless, couples might experience challenges related to previous decisions made as a result of extended family pressure. "George's parents really put a lot of pressure on us before we got engaged to ensure that we'd baptize our future children in the Greek Church. At the time, this seemed like a good compromise in order to keep the peace. But now that our children are eight and ten, I sometimes resent them and kick myself for yielding so readily to this pressure." In these cases, it is important to identify the source of the problem and seek to remedy it without placing blame. In addition, while boundaries between extended families and nuclear families have been drawn, couples need to be aware that extended family members might attempt to challenge these boundaries. They should remember that even though grandparents may be well-meaning, they need to stand together at these times, and respectfully remind extended family that they, as parents, will make decisions about their children's religious development and well-being. One respondent's comments make this point. "Hector's parents know that our children are Greek Orthodox. They also know that Greek Orthodox aren't permitted to receive Communion in non-Orthodox churches. So when I heard that they were bringing our children to the Roman Catholic Church and encouraging them to take Communion, I became very upset. It's not that I think the Roman Catholic Church is bad or anything like that, it's only that they should have asked us before doing this. But it's not a problem now. We worked things out. They agreed to ask us about things like this before doing anything."

• Finally, couples should remember that when inter-Christian families experience these challenges, most report working through them and emerging unscathed. Prayer and Christian understanding go a long way toward helping couples reach a healthy resolution. A respondent who had been married less than five years stated, "When we've been challenged, I remember the saying, 'when there is no way out, there is always a way up.' Prayer and respectful religious conversation has really helped us get around some of our problems because we're both really religious."

When Children Reach Adolescence

> "If teens know that both parents are in disagreement about an issue– and believe me they usually know – they will take advantage of this every time. When it comes to religion, I'm glad that we understood this before our kids reached their teens. We decided early on to get on the same page with regard to religion and educate ourselves so that we could participate in our children's religious education. If we hadn't done this, I'm certain our teens' feeling about God and religion would have suffered. Parents who belong to different churches need to be especially aware of this."
>
> Focus Group Respondent

When children reach adolescence, growth hormones promote numerous physiological changes. Their bodies are maturing, more sleep is required, and mood swings are common. Along with these biological changes, children's cognitive abilities increase and their capacity to conceptualize abstract concepts expand. These changes provoke independent thinking, numerous questions and some experimentation. Peer groups and our society's teen culture also take on greater importance in their lives.

Familial boundaries tend to become more fluid at this time in the family life cycle. For example, as adolescents desire increased amounts of independence and the latitude to make more of their own decisions, shifts occur in the way parents and adolescents interrelate. A constant negotiation process is occurring between teens and their parents, as parents seek to relinquish age appropriate, healthy amounts of independence to their teens.

Together with these typical challenges, intermarried families are prone to encountering some unique challenges. The following information identifies some of these challenges. A review and familiarity of this information should help you in your work with intermarried families with adolescents.

• Early family of origin experiences tend to play an important role in both an adolescent's impressions about culture and religion, as well as their continuing efforts to develop a cultural and religious identity. Prolonged indifference on the part of one or both spouses can negatively impact their children's religious and cultural development, as can consistent conflict. The following remarks illustrate these points. "Bill is not a very religious person. I think his lack of enthusiasm and our constant bickering back and forth about religion, especially on Sunday mornings, took a toll on our kids' religious commitment. Even though Bill's attitude has softened these past few years, and we've stopped arguing as often and as intensely, I'm afraid it was too little and too late. Now that our children are teens, I can't get them to come to church with me. And when I do manage to get them there, I can tell they don't really have much of an attachment to the church. Maybe some of this is because they are teens, but I can't help thinking that some of it has something to do with our many arguments and inability to agree about religion and culture when they were younger."

• Adolescence is a time when everything in life is questioned, including culture and religion. As a result, intermarried parents should expect their teenagers to both scrutinize and question their parents' cultural and religious values and beliefs. Parents who lack knowledge about their respective religious traditions, who have conflicted feelings over their religious and cultural differences, will likely fail miserably at addressing their adolescent's religious questions and needs. One father stated, "When we were young, we just accepted what our parents believed without too much argument. Things are different today. Kids today tend to question everything – especially when they are teens.... If you want your teens to respect what you believe, you'd better know how to answer their questions and complaints.... Today parents have to be in agreement – especially intermarried parents. They've also got to know a lot more about their faith if they expect to answer their teens' questions."

• If adolescents are raised in an intercultural, mixed-church family environment that is conflicted over culture and religion, and this conflict persists unchecked, then it is significantly more probable that they will reject the value of culture and religion altogether, or be influenced by their peers' perceptions of culture and religion. The following remarks from one focus group participant support this observation. "Religion isn't that important in our family. We hardly ever go to church, except to attend family functions and maybe on Easter or near Christmas. We decided early on that we wouldn't allow religion to create conflict in our home like it did in our childhood homes. So, we've always encouraged our children to think for themselves about issues like religion. Our two young adults have chosen not to attend a church, and that's okay with us. Our teenage daughter occasionally goes to her friend's church."

• Parents must remember that actions speak louder than words. When parents fail to celebrate their cultural differences or live out their religious beliefs, their children's religious and cultural development will generally be negatively impacted. "Jesus taught by example," stated one respondent. "You can't preach one thing and do another when it comes to religion. Your teens will see through this every time." If teenagers discern that their parents are saying one thing to them regarding the value of religion and culture, and demonstrating another, their efforts to develop a strong religious and cultural identity will be negatively impacted.

• Intermarried parents who have a sound understanding of each other's religious tradition, and are generally in agreement about religious matters, are in a better position to address the adolescent's religious questions. Parents, who have been in agreement about their religious and cultural differences and have offered clear messages to their children regarding religion and culture, will likely encounter fewer and less intense challenges. One mother's remarks supports this observation. "Despite our religious differences, our daughters have always known that we are on the same page when it comes to church attendance.... Our youngest tried to test the waters and tried to question regular church attendance when she was about thirteen. She wanted to stay home like her friends and sleep – teens tend to do a lot of sleeping. So, she started testing us to see if she could get us to bend the rules. But we held firm, and let her know that this was not an option in our home. She grumbled a little bit at first, and dragged her feet, but then accepted our rule. It was tough for a few years, but now that she's eighteen, I think she is beginning to develop a feeling for God and her religious background. If we had yielded to her complaints a few years back, I'm sure she wouldn't have as deep a feeling for her Christian and Orthodox background."

• Permitting adolescents the latitude to question religious beliefs can prove to be a necessary part of their efforts to personalize their religious beliefs. Inter-Christian parents should welcome questions from their adolescents, and view their questions as opportunities for all members of the family to develop a deeper cultural and religious identity. "At first, I was concerned when the questions about religion started coming, because we didn't know very much about our faith. But we didn't get rattled. We decided to view the questions as an opportunity for growth. With our priest's help and the reading that we did, our teen's questions about religion proved helpful to the entire family's religious development."

• Inter-Christian parents must try to help their adolescents develop a respect for other faith groups while also helping them to grow into a personal faith commitment in the church where they were baptized. As one parent stated, "We live in a multi-religious society. It doesn't do parents any good to argue with their teens about which religion is better. It seems to me that this is the wrong way to go. I think you need to help your teens respect other religions, while also helping them embrace their own religious background.... It's hard, but not impossible.... That's where the church can help us." When parents remind adolescents that they are part of a rich religious tradition that can facilitate a meaningful relationship with God, this positive emphasis assists them in discerning the value and worth of being religious. If parents spend most of their time disparaging other religions and cultural groups, such activity may simply serve to reduce adolescents' respect for their religious and cultural heritage.

• Research also suggests that if only one parent has a strong cultural and religious identity, then it is probable that adolescents will embrace the dominant parent's cultural and religious preferences. "I'm the religious one, so our children are Greek Orthodox," stated one respondent. "And I hope that they continue with their faith. But there are no guarantees. I know that they might one day choose another religion. But I hope not." Adolescents who tended to identify with only one parent's cultural background may at a later stage in life discover and search out information about the other parent's cultural and religious background.

• Couples who have been conflicted over their religious and cultural differences for some time will often feel a sense of failure when their children approach adolescence. Some may even be inclined to blame themselves or one another for their children's indifference toward religion. Feelings of regret and loss may also be experienced. These feelings and thoughts can contribute to marital dissatisfaction and family disunity. In most instances, such couples may not be entirely conscious of the undermining effects of these feelings and thoughts until after the children have left home. In other cases, these feelings and thoughts may be constant irritants that lie smoldering and unattended until an argument occurs. When conflict occurs, they can ignite and add to couple conflict and family instability.

When Children Begin Leaving Home

> "A friend of mine approached me one day and started complaining because her daughter had decided to attend some Evangelical Church. I tried consoling her, by telling her that she is still young and will likely come back to the Greek Church. But all the while I was really thinking, what did you expect, you hardly ever brought her to church. I felt guilty about thinking this way, especially since I know that her husband's indifference toward religion was probably a big reason why this happened."
>
> Focus Group Participant

When children in our culture reach young adulthood, they are well on their way toward completing the individuation process[69] from their family of origin. In addition, parents are generally busy assisting and supporting them in their efforts to individuate. Young adults and parents are also actively retooling the nature of their relationships, forming more symmetrical relationships (adult to adult) and less complimentary relationships (adult to child). While most active parenting duties are over at this juncture, young adults still have needs and parents continue to offer them support.

Along with the challenges that single-church families encounter, results from the IRP suggest that inter-Christian and intercultural families are predisposed to experience additional challenges linked to their religious and cultural differences. The following observations and insights should help you gain a deeper appreciation of these unique challenges.

• When young adults do separate, they tend to separate from their family of origin, as well as the cultural, religious, and community structures of their youth. This does not necessarily imply that young adults will discard their cultural and religious roots since in most cases this does not happen. Young adults are simply creating enough space between themselves and their parents to afford themselves ample room to make independent choices and decisions about important matters such as culture and religion. In other instances, the value of religion and their ethnic background will not become apparent to them until after marriage and when they have their own families. One respondent's observations are typical of many young adults. "When I left home, you might say I also left my church and culture. And I didn't really return until I was settled and sort of looking to settle down. Organized religion seemed irrelevant to my needs. Of course, all that's changed now."

• Many parents have a hard time relinquishing control and cultivating an adult-to-adult relationship with their children at this time. Many will seek to control, threaten and manipulate their young adult children's decisions. Some of this may have something to do with a clash of cultural norms and intergenerational differences. As one parent stated, "Things have really changed from the time I was growing up in Greece and what it's like in America today. If I had acted like our daughter does, my father would have brained me. Today parents have to be flexible. Otherwise they will move out and do whatever they please." If parents are too intrusive and seek to impose their values on their young adult children, they may cause tension or a cutoff to occur between the young adult and themselves. One respondent stated, "I have minimal contact with my parents. That's because they've refused to accept my African American wife. It's been almost twelve years and this issue still divides us. It saddens me, but I've kind of accepted the fact that things may never change. They are so stubborn."

• Parents with strong opinions about religion can potentially drive a wedge between themselves and their children. Young adult children might pretend to espouse certain religious and ethnic affiliations to please their parents. "I've always gone to the Greek Church to please my parents," stated one respondent. "Quite frankly I don't understand it, and don't have the time to try. So, we go once in a while to appease my parents." They might also resent covert and overt intrusions into this part of their lives that could negatively color their relationship.

"Mind you now, I was almost twenty-five when this happened," stated another focus group participant. "One Sunday when my mother was giving me the third degree about not being in church – she's a very religious woman – I told her to lay off or I'd stop coming around on Sundays. I really felt bad about this. But enough was enough. She has her way of thinking and I have mine." In some instances, temporary or permanent cut-offs might also take place when irreconcilable value differences exist between a parent(s) and a young adult child. "It's really silly, but my folks and I didn't talk for nearly one year when I was about 23. And it was over religion. Things have changed. I've come to understand the value of religion as I had children and I guess my parents also mellowed out about this issue."

• As young adult children appear to be making decisions about religion and culture, it can be a particularly unsettling time for all members of the nuclear family. If parents have not come to terms with their religious differences, old wounds will generally surface and irritate their marriage — especially if their adult children make decisions about religion that appear to be related to parents' unresolved religious differences. In this case, couples might be prone to assign blame and reopen old arguments. One respondent stated, "Yes, I blamed him and he blamed me for our daughter's interest in a cult – the name of the group isn't important.... We hardly ever see her, because the group's leaders don't allow her to have much contact with us. We wonder what it might have been like if we all attended one church. Sometimes I believe that she did this because of the religious and cultural wars that we engaged in due to our religious and cultural differences. We're really trying to prevent this from happening to our other two teenagers."

• Unlike adolescents who busy themselves experimenting and testing out new ideas, most young adults are beginning to form the basis of a solid and stable life structure and cultural identity which will ultimately assist them in their efforts to make crucial decisions about their career and future mate. While many may not seem religious, research suggests that young adults generally rely on the moral and value structure they inherited from their family of origin to begin making important decisions[70].

• Finally, there are many reasons why young adults who have been raised in an inter-Christian and intercultural home eventually identify with a given church and culture. In general, their decision can be linked to family of origin experiences and peer group influences. Moreover, most young adults can be grouped into one of the following four categories.[71]

1. Some young adults will primarily be labeled "majority group identifiers" and tend to identify with the parent who is from the dominant culture. These individuals may or may not identify with the other parent who is from a minority culture.

2. Some young adults will be labeled "minority group identifiers" and essentially identify with the minority ethnic, racial, or religious background of one of his or her parents. In these instances, the young adult may or may not acknowledge the other parent's background.

3. Some young adults will embrace a "universalizes/disaffiliates: none of the above" attitude toward culture and religion, and tend to create their own values, rituals and identity irrespective of their parent's cultural and religious backgrounds. These young adults may refuse to accept any labels or create a distinct label that differentiates them from any childhood cultural and religious labels.

4. Some young adults are "synthesizers." These young adults strive to bring together and integrate both their parents' cultural and religious backgrounds. They acknowledge that both their parents have influenced their perceptions of culture and religion.

After the Last Child has Left Home

> "Sometimes, in my weakest moments, I look back and wonder what it might have been like if I married a Greek. Please don't get me wrong, we love each other and I am committed to my husband. He is a good man, and a fine provider. But over the years he never really understood how important my heritage is to me. And now that I'm getting older,

my background is playing a more prominent role in the way I see things. I guess it saddens me that I can't share this part of my life with the person with whom I am sharing my life."

Focus Group Respondent

When the last child has finally left home, a couple's focus will shift back to the marriage. While most couples will make a smooth transition into this stage and find it an exciting and fulfilling time, some will encounter challenges. For instance, couples who have been thoroughly absorbed in raising their children might suddenly become aware that they do not know each other. These couples might question the viability of their marriages. In these instances, unattended couple issues that have lain dormant for years because parents have been focused on children's needs, might suddenly surface with renewed vigor to unsettle spouses and couples. Gender differences also challenge couples. Men are generally seeking to slow down and tend to become more nurturing and domesticated while many women may be interested in making their mark on the world by starting a career.

It is no wonder that many couples who reach this point might experience a kind of midlife marriage burnout[72]. Together with these kinds of growing pains, intermarried couples may encounter some unique challenges related to their different religious and cultural backgrounds. This section will seek to introduce you to some of the unique couple challenges these couples might encounter during the stage of marriage that is often termed the "empty nest."

• If a couple was conflicted over their religious and cultural differences before the children arrived, and they were unable to resolve their differences, they may resurface at this time. The following observations exemplify this point. "For years, it was always me and the children on Sundays. As the children grew and began to have their own lives, I started trying to convince my husband to come to church with me. But he had his own preferences on Sunday mornings, and going to my church wasn't high on his list. I tried to reason with him, but he wouldn't change his mind. So, for a while I stopped going to church regularly, because I didn't want to go alone. I would just stay home and silently resent him. Then I thought to myself, why am I doing this. If he doesn't want to go, well that's fine, but look what this issue is doing to you and your marriage. So, I started attending more regularly alone.... It still bothers me when I think about his indifference toward organized religion, but I have learned to respect it for the sake of our relationship."

• As was mentioned above, individuals tend to review their lives at this juncture in the life cycle. If lost opportunities and poor decisions were made earlier, many will wonder what things might have been like if they had made other decisions. Along these lines, spouses who have struggled with lingering unresolved issues related to their religious and cultural differences might look back and either wonder what it might have been like if he or she had married someone from the same faith and or ethnic background. A respondent confided the following to me after a focus group: "This may sound crazy, because I've been married twenty years. These days I sometimes find myself wondering what it might have been like if I had dated more Greek girls.... I'm not going to act on anything, but I wonder what that kind of a life might have been like. I guess it's natural for people to wonder about these things, especially because we've never been able to agree about religion and our cultural differences."

• In some instances, spouses who have failed to resolve and negotiate their cultural and religious differences may consider worshipping in different churches and, or renewing cultural ties that have been ignored for years while raising their children. In a few instances, some couples' religious and cultural differences may prompt one or both spouses to consider separation and divorce once the last child has left home. With the previous focus on their children gone, some couples may even question the value and wisdom of remaining in a relationship that is conflicted over religion and culture. As one individual whom I corresponded with via e-mail stated, "We've been married for thirty years, and we've been worshipping in the Greek Orthodox Church all this time. Recently, after our last son relocated to another part of the country, my wife tells me she wants to go back to the Baptist Church because she's never felt comfortable in the Greek Orthodox Church. Well, that really made me mad and sad.... Since I won't consider going to the Baptist Church, we are now going in separate directions every Sunday. This has hurt me deeply. I feel like our marriage has lost something." Those who do not pursue a divorce will not merely report experiencing dissatisfaction with their marriages, but will also report feelings of loneliness and symptoms of depression that will negatively affect individual well-being.

• These lingering cultural and religious differences can also function to negatively influence their children's and grandchildren's attitudes and perceptions of religion and ethnicity. "When I look back at our many disagreements over religion these past twenty-five years," stated one IRP participant in a melancholy tone. "I know that these disagreements have not only affected me, but have also affected our children's attitude about religion. I expect that this will have an impression on our grandchildren's attitudes."

• In cases where couples appear to be caught within these types of irreconcilable differences, experience suggests that matters will not improve. However, all is not lost and change can occur if both desire change. Turning to God and allowing Him to remove their seemingly immovable difficulties is crucial at this time. Where their own efforts have proven inadequate, God's forgiveness, mercy, and love can loosen things up and allow them to view their differences from another perspective. As God's life-changing grace touches their lives, behavioral changes can occur that serve to improve individual, couple, and family well-being.

Two Ways to Present This Information to Intermarried Couples

From this resource, I hope that you have come to realize that most intermarried couples struggle with numerous challenges that single-church couples do not encounter. Since most intermarried couples I have worked with appreciate the opportunity to discuss these challenges with other intermarried couples, I am presenting two suggested formats to help you facilitate this process. One way of presenting this information is to invite a speaker to conduct a marriage-building retreat. As part of the retreat, the speaker could consider intermarried couple challenges. This experience should also afford couples the opportunity to gather in groups of three or four couples. These groups would be given some open-ended questions like those listed below to encourage a group dialogue. A second approach might be to invite a few intermarried couples to present some of their challenges in a panel discussion format. These couples should also be familiar with the materials in this chapter. After the panel discussion, breakout groups would be structured as I have described above.

- What has it been like being intermarried?
- What expected and unexpected challenges have you encountered?
- How have these challenges impacted your marital satisfaction and family stability?
- How have these challenges impacted your children's religious and spiritual development?
- What kinds of balancing strategies have you used to address these challenges? (For instance, some couples report that prayer has helped them find some balance when they encountered a challenge related to their different religious or cultural backgrounds.)

• What advice would you share with engaged couples who are contemplating intermarriage?

• How has your faith in Christ helped you address your challenges?

Guidelines That Should Assist Clergy and Lay Workers

In most cases, intermarried couples will eventually either reach a mutually satisfying resolution or simply learn to live with the challenges described above. Some may also consult you for a second opinion in their efforts to resolve these issues. If they do, usually a supportive, prayerful shoulder to lean on is all most will need to help them work through their challenges. Reminding them that their faith in God can help them, and offering them some useful observations and information will generally help them find some answers and overcome their challenges[73].

Occasionally, your counsel may be sought for challenges of a more complex and serious nature. These types of challenges will likely resemble pervasive problems that have grown and festered over time and are undermining marital satisfaction and family stability and may be linked to their religious and cultural differences. If you are approached with these types of challenges, the following guidelines should prove helpful as you seek to provide some consolation and assistance[74].

As I have suggested in earlier chapters, when a conflicted spouse approaches you for help, try not to under or overestimate your expertise. You have some valuable experience and knowledge to share. However, you should also remember to recognize your limitations. Please also remember that issues of a serious nature will require more time and attention. At minimum, serious problems will likely require you to meet with the individual or couple a minimum of 4 to 10 one hour weekly sessions.[75] If your schedule does not permit this kind of commitment, or if you do not feel comfortable doing this type of work, it might be better that you admit this to both yourself and the spouse or couple and offer a referral.

Should you elect to try and help, before offering any substantive counsel, remember what scripture counsels, "Let every man be quick to hear, and slow to speak" (JM 1:19). In other words, you should listen carefully to the details of the individual or couple's story before offering substantive feedback.

Remaining as neutral as possible throughout this process is also important. Since you will be required to offer information that supports the Orthodox Church's position,[76] you will find it difficult, if not impossible, to retain a neutral position at all times. As such, qualifying your remarks at the outset with statements like, "I'm in an awkward position here. I want to help you both resolve your differences, but I must also respect the Orthodox Church's pastoral guidelines. So, at times I might sound as though I am siding with the Greek Orthodox partner. In actuality, I simply want to respect the Orthodox Church's pastoral guidelines while trying to help you both arrive at some holy and healthy decisions. So, if either of you feel as if I am being unfair, don't hesitate to tell me how you are feeling." Such observations may also help you avoid being unwittingly recruited into a coalition by the Greek Orthodox partner against the non-Orthodox mate. Please remember, your neutrality will be key to your efforts to help facilitate some positive, holy change.

If after hearing the presenting problem(s) you feel some discomfort, it would not be inappropriate to share this with the spouse or couple. During this part of the counseling process, it would also be a good idea to reexamine the pros and cons of a referral. Questions like the following few should be addressed: How do you feel about proceeding with counseling given some of my discomfort? Perhaps you might be better served if I offered a referral, what do you think? As you discuss this option, remember that all individuals involved in counseling should feel comfortable with the counseling arrangement – both the couple and you. During this discussion, you should also inform the individual or couple that if a referral appears to be the best course of action, such a decision would not necessarily preclude you from remaining part of the healing process so that you can offer religious and spiritual support. Should you discern that a referral is not necessary, the following additional guidelines will be of further assistance.

As I have previously indicated, many of the serious issues you will hear will be related to developmental and subsystem challenges. (For more information regarding this last statement, review the materials in Chapter 7.) By prayerfully helping the spouse or couple conceptualize their challenge(s) from a developmental, systems perspective, new and different ways of viewing and resolving the challenge(s) will likely emerge. If this pastoral approach does not begin to prove helpful in a few sessions, you might again consider revisiting the idea of a referral.

At this juncture of the counseling process you should be seeking to help couples discern how their religious and cultural differences have created lingering problems. Helping spouses and couples prayerfully discuss some of the regrets, fears and frustrations that they have encountered as intermarried couples in an effort to facilitate empathy and understanding should be a primary objective during this part of counseling. In addition, helping them discern how God and a Christian perspective of marriage can be helpful is an equally important objective. This part of counseling must help spouses and couples develop more respect for their differences and similarities, while also helping them reframe their differences in a positive light that has the potential to enrich their lives as individuals, couples and a family.

Additionally, at some juncture during this process you may be led to conclude that the spouse or couple might profit from some conversation related to the pros and cons of becoming a single-church couple. If this option appears to be a healthy option that the couple or individual might carefully examine, it would not be inappropriate for you to respectfully explore this subject. One way to help you introduce this subject is to tell them that you would like to offer some information that might prove helpful. If the couple is receptive, I generally offer the following observations.

• Let the couple know that you have their best interests in mind and are not trying to push them into making a decision that is either untimely or inappropriate. Let them also know that if they have any questions regarding what you are about to present, you would be happy to discuss their questions at any time. Assure them that you are simply offering this option because you feel this may prove helpful to them in their efforts to resolve their present challenges(s). Let them also know that you believe this is a personal issue that must be considered prayerfully. You might then consider reviewing some of the materials in Chapters 4 and 5. You should also suggest the materials in Chapters 3 and 4 in the intermarried couples resource.

• Let them also know that many intermarried couples who have previously not argued about their religious differences, may find themselves embroiled in conflict over their differences when the children arrive or as their children are maturing. In addition, tell them that research indicates that many of these couples decide to become single-church couples for the sake of their children and family.[77] Let them also know that the challenges that they have described are typical challenges that intermarried couples encounter. This strategy will serve to normalize their problems, minimize their fears and anxiety and facilitate better understanding. You should also determine to review the materials in Chapter 6 in the couples' resource entitled, "Parenting Challenges."

As you seek to help, remember the old adage, "You can win the battle, but lose the war." In other words, if the counseling process does not allow the couple the latitude to arrive at their own decisions, you may have unintentionally created more problems than you resolved. The rule of thumb is to respectfully and prayerfully provide couples with information that will allow them the latitude to make their own decisions. Should they request your opinion, I would offer them your thoughts with the following caveat attached: "I appreciate your asking for my thoughts, but remember, the final decision must always be yours."

Summary

This chapter was written to acquaint you with some of the unique developmental and systemic challenges that intermarried couples encounter. I have provided you with some suggestions to present these materials to the intermarried couples in your parish. The key components of a pastoral approach that I find to be effective were also outlined. As you acquaint yourself with these materials, I pray they will be helpful to you in your own efforts to minister more effectively to the intermarried couples and their families in the parish you serve.

Chapter Twelve

Pastoral Directives[78]

Over the centuries, the Orthodox Church has essentially held to the position that intra-Orthodox marriages are strongly preferred to inter-Christian and inter-religious marriages for the following three reasons.[79] First, Scripture tends to support intra-faith marriage and rejects inter-religious marriage. Second, the Church has determined that intra-Orthodox marriages have a more favorable impact on the well-being of both spouse's religious and spiritual development as compared to inter-Christian and inter-religious marriages. Third, by supporting intra-Orthodox marriages, the Church believes that it will ensure its continued survival at both a micro (parish level) and macro level (Diocesan, Archdiocesan and Patriarchal levels).

As a result, a number of canons have been promulgated over the centuries to bolster these positions. These canons serve either to discourage inter-Christian, inter-religious marriages or condemn them. The promulgation of these canons does not, however, suggest that Orthodox Christians were completely dissuaded from engaging in inter-Christian, inter-religious marriages, since historical evidence indicates otherwise.

With the steady increase in the number of intermarriages occurring between Orthodox Christians and non-Orthodox around the world, the Church has tended to modify its position regarding inter-Christian marriages through the use of *economia*,[80] i.e., a type of theological tolerance which is sometimes utilized for pastoral reasons. Depending on the perceived pastoral needs of a given autocephalous Orthodox Church,[81] more leniency has been shown toward inter-Christian marriages and inter-religious marriages throughout the Orthodox world.

For example, "The Russian and other Orthodox Churches in Europe and the Near East do not refuse the Sacraments to an Orthodox spouse married to a non-Orthodox, [or] even to a non-Christian" (Constantelos, 1997, p. 69).[82] Finally, since the Greek Orthodox Archdiocese falls under the direct jurisdiction of the Ecumenical Patriarchate, Constantinople decidedly impacts the position of the Greek Orthodox Archdiocese toward intermarriages.

Pastoral Directives

The following pastoral directives function to guide and facilitate the Greek Orthodox priests' work with couples who either are contemplating an inter-Christian, interchurch marriage or are presently involved in an inter-Christian, interchurch marriage. These directives flow out of the Orthodox Church's understanding of marriage and its desire to assist its marriages and families in their efforts to cultivate (with God's grace) an Orthodox Christian environment in their homes.

As a result of the Orthodox concept of *economia,* inter-Christian marriages between an Orthodox Christian and another Trinitarian Christian are now permitted. Briefly, the Church has made this concession because it recognizes that we live in an increasingly pluralistic society. The Church is also concerned with each member's salvation, and therefore does not desire to place any obstacle before its faithful by denying the Sacrament of Marriage to those who choose to enter an inter-Christian marriage.

Although the Orthodox Church has determined to permit inter-Christian marriages between its faithful and other Trinitarian Christians, it has done so by seeking to protect its theological integrity. To that end, the following additional pastoral directives (regarding inter-Christian marriages between Orthodox Christians and other Trinitarian Christians) have emerged.

Since the Sacrament of Marriage is a Christian ceremony, and the Orthodox Church does not perform the Sacrament of Marriage for an Orthodox Christian and an un-baptized person, non-Orthodox Christians wishing to get married in the Orthodox Church must have been baptized in the name of the Holy Trinity. In addition, the Orthodox Church also does not perform the Sacrament of Marriage for two non-Orthodox Christians. At least one individual must be Orthodox in good standing[83] with his or her parish.

In order to remain in proper canonical and spiritual standing with the Orthodox Church, Orthodox Christians must be married by an Orthodox priest, in an Orthodox Church, and in the manner prescribed by the priest's service book.

Couples marrying in the Orthodox Church must also commit themselves to baptizing and raising their children in the Orthodox Church. Orthodox Christians who choose to baptize their future children in their partner's church call into question their desire to live an Orthodox lifestyle. Such a decision affects the Orthodox partner's standing with his or her church.

Since only Orthodox Christians are permitted to participate in the Orthodox Church's sacraments, sponsors exchanging the wedding rings and crowns must be Orthodox Christians in good standing with their parish. This rule is connected to the church's understanding of the sponsor. Briefly, the sponsor is more than a legal witness. The sponsor also functions as a spokesperson for the Orthodox congregation affirming the spiritual preparedness of the couple to enter into the community of marriage.

Orthodox partners should be made aware that if their marriage is not solemnized by the Orthodox Church, they are no longer in good standing and are not permitted to receive the sacraments or participate in the sacraments as a sponsor.[84]

Double performances of the wedding service, that is, in both the Orthodox Church and another Church are not encouraged. This guideline is relaxed when an Orthodox Christian has been married outside of the Orthodox Church and wishes to return to the Orthodox Church and once again become canonically and spiritually in good standing with his or her Church. In this case, after the Orthodox priest receives permission from his bishop, the Sacrament of Marriage is performed.

Co-celebrations of the Sacrament of Marriage between Orthodox and non-Orthodox clergy are not permitted. While non-Orthodox clergy are not permitted to co-celebrate the Sacrament of Marriage with the Orthodox priest they may attend and offer a benediction to the couple as well as prayerful words of exhortation.

Inter-Christian couples who wish the presence of a non-Orthodox clergyman during the Sacrament of Marriage should make their desire known to the Orthodox pastor. He will then seek the Bishop's permission. Interchurch couples should also be made aware of the following additional procedures.

• The Orthodox priest will extend an invitation to the non-Orthodox clergyman. At that time, the Orthodox priest will respectfully state that a co-celebration of the Sacrament of Marriage is not permitted since the Orthodox Church does not permit non-Orthodox clergy to participate in the sacraments.

• The Orthodox priest will also clearly advise the guest clergyman on matters of appropriate vesture and seating (which is generally located in a prominent place on the *Solea)*. Additionally, he will also clearly indicate that the guest clergy will be properly acknowledged and permitted to give a benediction, and address the couple with some words, good wishes, and an exhortation at the conclusion of the Sacrament of Marriage.

• The couple should also be told that wedding invitations and newspaper announcements must clearly distinguish between the Orthodox celebrant and the guest clergy. Terms like "assisted" or "participated" should be avoided. Optional descriptors such as "was present" or "was present and subsequently gave a blessing" should be selected and utilized so as to clearly describe the non-Orthodox visiting cleric's role. In addition, Orthodox priests who are invited to attend non-Orthodox wedding services may only attend as guests.

Intermarried couples are also respectfully informed that non-Orthodox Christians who marry in the Orthodox Church do not subsequently have sacramental privileges in the Orthodox Church. Because of the Orthodox Church's position on sacramental participation, only those who are in good standing canonically and spiritually have sacramental privileges. Similarly, intermarried couples should also be aware that only Orthodox Christians who are in good standing canonically and spiritually are (a) permitted an Orthodox Funeral Service, (b) allowed to serve on the Parish Council, (c) permitted to vote in parish elections, and (d) permitted to serve as godparents or sponsors at baptisms and weddings.

Chapter Thirteen

Pastoral Approaches And Programs

It should come as no surprise that the Church cannot possibly attend to every need and expectation that intermarried couples have. Many of the changes that intermarried couples would like the Church to institute either conflict with Orthodox theology or may take an extended period of time to resolve. For instance, many inter-Christian couples would like their non-Orthodox spouses to have access to Holy Communion. Many of these same couples would also like non-Orthodox extended family members to be able to function as godparents and sponsors. These perceived needs require careful examination, and are simply untenable at this time for numerous theological and historical reasons. "A lot more English, and a lot less Greek," is also another frequent request that intermarried couples make. But in some communities an attempt to drastically alter the ratio of Greek to English may create more conflict than it resolves. "The ability to vote and assume leadership positions," is also frequently mentioned. Yet, this proposal needs very careful review and may well be untenable for theological reasons, especially when related to the parish council.

Striking a balance between what changes intermarried couples would like instituted, what changes our local congregations are prepared to embrace, and what changes fit with our theology often appears to be a somewhat elusive proposition, but not an impossibility with God's help. As you will note from reading this chapter's contents, some changes can be implemented almost immediately, while others will require prayerful forethought and some careful examination. With God's help and guidance, and in God's good time, I believe the tenuous balance between intermarried couples needs, local church needs and our efforts to protect Orthodox theological integrity will prayerfully emerge.

In addition, geographic idiosyncrasies, and local community needs and limitations will impact the types of programs and approaches that are implemented from one community to the next. For example, some churches located in large urban areas who service several thousand families, will need to develop more formal ways to reach out to its intermarried couples. In these types of communities, intermarriage committees, intermarriage groups, retreats, seminars and the recruitment of mentor couples might thus be considered to begin meeting these needs. Small churches may not necessarily have a need to become as formalized and sophisticated, and might develop a less structured and more individualized approach. In either case, reaching out to this growing population is imperative, and must be considered in some form if we are to keep these couples, families and their children from drifting away from the Orthodox Church.[85]

Finally, the information in this chapter is not anecdotal in nature, i.e., the result of a few individuals' experiences and opinions. The following suggestions have been systematically distilled from hundreds of intermarried spouses' observations, together with numerous clergy who were asked open-ended questions. Respondents' comments were then subsequently collapsed and organized to produce the information that follows. The value of proceeding in this manner, is that the observations and approaches included below have a higher probability of resonating with the intermarried couples in your parish, since they emerged directly from intermarried couples and clergy who minister to them. As you begin working and reworking the information that follows to fit your local needs, I have no doubt that successful intermarriage ministries will emerge that will function to provide further guidance and example to us all.

What are some basic realities that the Church must consider in its efforts to minister to intermarried couples?

• The church is embedded in an inclusive, pluralistic society that is extremely sensitive to issues of diversity and multiculturalism. As such, the Greek Orthodox Church of America (GOA) must seek to determine – at both a macro and micro level – how this impacts its own mission and role. If the GOA ignores the diverse ethnic and religious social milieu in which the Church exists, and espouses and promotes exclusive, ethnocentric and nationalistic perspectives, results from the IRP suggest that this approach will provide intermarried couples with the impression that the Church is irrelevant, insensitive, and out-of-step with contemporary couple and family needs. That is because intermarried couples – not unlike most members of our society – tend to espouse an inclusive view of the world that values, respects, tolerates, and accepts "difference." Another reason is because intermarried couples have personally dealt with their own ethnic and religious differences, and have seen how respect and tolerance for difference has enriched their lives as individuals, couples, and families. Therefore, they tend to believe that tolerance, acceptance, and respect for difference is not only important to their own families, but is critical to the social stability of a pluralistic society like our own. As such, churches that embrace such a perspective, while also not compromising Orthodox theology, will tend to be more successful in ministering to this population of faithful.

• If a Greek Orthodox Church sends overt or covert ethnocentric, nationalistic messages to its faithful that not only applaud Hellenism's accomplishments, but also serve to disparage other ethnic and religious traditions, such an approach alienates intermarried couples. Such messages are like a double-edged sword. While celebrating Hellenism, they tend to disparage other ethnic and religious traditions and inhibit our efforts to gather intermarried couples and families into the fold. If the GOA (at all levels) is to succeed in making more meaningful connections with intermarried couples, one important approach it must take is to label ethnocentric, nationalistic attitudes as "unacceptable and inappropriate." We can still celebrate Hellenism's contributions to society, since intermarried couples value America's ethnic richness and diversity, but not at the expense of other religious and ethnic traditions. Finding this delicate balance is not an easy task, but it is necessary in our efforts to reach out to this growing population of faithful.[86]

• Coupled with these observations, local clergy and lay leaders must seek to cultivate positive attitudes for the diversity that exists within their Greek Orthodox community. Clergy and lay leaders must acknowledge the fact that our churches are rapidly becoming populated with faithful from different backgrounds who have diverse needs. To be more specific, we are a Church that is increasingly being populated with persons from a non-Greek ethnic and mixed ethnic background. That being the case, we must begin granting more than tacit approval to this reality and find ways of cultivating these changes. Such an approach will begin meeting more of the needs of all the faithful who choose to worship in the GOA.

How can the Church be more welcoming to the non-Orthodox spouse?

• Up until recently, our Churches were generally populated by faithful who had a decidedly Greek Orthodox background. For this reason, most of the programs and approaches were intended to meet the needs of Greek Orthodox Christians with a Greek background. My research suggests that as the composition of the faithful praying in our churches has begun to change, our local church programs and approaches to non-Orthodox have not kept pace. Numerous Greek Orthodox faithful have strongly begun to urge their local church to find creative ways to include non-Orthodox (and their families) into its religious and social life without necessarily violating the church's canons and, or being disrespectful to its Hellenic background. One non-Greek Orthodox respondent's words are typical of how many non-Greek Orthodox feel about this. "I have an Anglo-Saxon background, but when I come to the Greek Orthodox Church I feel as if I have to hide that side of me. And while that's usually okay with me, I wonder how healthy that might be to the Greek Church's efforts to attract and keep non-Greek Orthodox plugged into its religious and social life." By finding new and creative ways of including non-Greek Orthodox into its social and religious fabric, we make it easier for them to meet their religious and social needs. We also increase the likelihood that intermarried couples may opt to attend our churches together and with more frequency.

• The church can also seek to find respectful ways to assist non-Orthodox spouses in their efforts to consider conversion. While it is true that many non-Orthodox spouses are non-Orthodox by choice, results from the IRP suggest that a small but sizable number of non-Greek Orthodox spouses (perhaps 10 – 20%) who attend our churches might consider conversion if they were respectfully approached with the idea at pivotal times during the life cycle. For instance, my research suggests that a good time is before couples wed. Other instances are when the first child arrives or when children begin attending Sunday School or before they reach ten years old. In the words of one non-Orthodox spouse, "Before Father John asked me to convert, I didn't feel as if the congregation was interested in having me become a part of the church. After he asked, I started thinking about it. I finally approached Father John in a few months and told him I was ready to enter the church." Some non-Greek Orthodox who attend our churches may hold to the perception that our churches are only for "Greeks." Respectful outreach to non-Orthodox through a number of different ways such as Inquirers Classes for non-Orthodox, sermons, and bulletin messages that encourage non-Orthodox conversion, might serve to dispel such notions, and help some intermarried couples meet their religious needs.

How can the Church assist intermarried parents?

• Just as single-church and single-cultural couples want the church to assist them in their efforts to inculcate their children with a moral and religious foundation, intermarried couples also desire the Church to help them with this parental responsibility. Sunday School programs, retreats, and Christ-centered youth groups that are designed to help their children develop a Christian moral and religious perspective tend to be of primary importance to this group of faithful. The following statement is indicative of the value these types of couples place on youth programs and religious education. Concerning the difficulties that face contemporary parents today, one respondent stated: "I don't want my children to be like one of these people out on the streets that do all kinds of stuff. The murders, the drugs, the alcohol, the teenage pregnancies – I don't want that for my children. I want them to become decent people with good morals – morals that keep you alive and out of trouble. I want the church to help me by being there to do it with me. I need more support. I need more help. That's the kind of church I want."

• When the Church fails to provide a Christ-centered youth program, many intermarried couples whose children have been baptized in the Greek Orthodox Church meet this need outside the Orthodox Church – often in the non-Orthodox spouses' faith community. For example, many intermarried couples might place their children in a non-Greek Orthodox parochial school, Summer Vacation Bible school, and Summer Christian Camp. Such decisions may not necessarily be construed in negative terms from the parent's point of view, but they should be of some concern to us. That is because research indicates one primary purpose that youth programs serve, is to help children identify and bond with a given faith community.[87] By working constantly to improve the church's youth program, the church will ensure that it is at once meeting some very important needs these couples, parents and their children have while also helping intermarried couple's children develop an attachment to their Greek Orthodox background.

• The Church can also assist intermarried couples by helping their children understand intermarriage. Generally speaking, church group activities and educational materials have failed to broach the subject of intermarriage with its children, or frequently send subtle messages to them that their non-Greek and non-Orthodox background is less important. In making this point, one respondent said, "The church has to be more sensitive to mixed faith families' needs. Yesterday my daughter's Sunday School teacher told the class that interfaith marriage is a sin.... Now how do you think my daughter felt.... She doesn't want to go back there again. I need the church's help. It's hard enough trying to keep my children committed to Orthodoxy without having to fight these kinds of battles. Please help me!" As such, while Sunday School materials may contain a balanced respect for Hellenism, and other ethnic backgrounds, Sunday School teachers might not always convey this message. Additionally, youth groups such as HOPE, JOY, GOYA and YAL should (a) respectfully acknowledge our faithful's religious and cultural diversity, (b) foster tolerance, acceptance, and respect for all those who worship in our churches, and (c) begin respectfully introducing adolescents to the complex topic of intermarriage.

• While intermarried couples value and respect Hellenism, they are not necessarily invested in acculturating their children into only one ethnic background. One intermarried parent's remarks are indicative of how most feel about ethnicity and culture. "Yes, I want my son and daughter to speak some Greek and develop a love of Greek music, but I also want them to know their Father's Guatemalan language and culture." In most instances, intermarried couples would like their children to be exposed to both parents' ethnic backgrounds because they believe that ethnicity enriches people's lives. As such, many desire and would likely support church programs and activities that afford intermarried couples the opportunity to expose their children to Greek culture. However, what makes many of these parents leery of these programs is if they happen to be overtly ethnocentric. My research shows that intermarried couples seldom object to Greek school and Greek dancing so long as respect for other cultural groups is maintained and promoted. The point is not that intermarried couples object to youth programs that promote Greek culture, because this is part of their family's heritage, but that some programs are exclusionary in nature.

What are some tangible approaches and programs that can assist intermarried couples?

In addition to what has been stated, the following suggestions may prove useful to you and the congregations you serve. They are offered respectfully and with the understanding that you are the best judge of what can and cannot work in your community.

• Local churches can provide premarital preparation that is uniquely tailored toward meeting the needs of intermarried couples. This process can respectfully help couples understand what inter-Christian and intercultural challenges they may encounter as (a) individuals, (b) spouses, and (c) families. Respectfully describing the pros and cons of remaining in an inter-Christian marriage as opposed to becoming a single-church couple should be a part of this process. (See Chapter 14 for more information).

• The local church might consider offering instructional classes and seminars for intermarried couples and the non-Orthodox spouse. The objective behind these classes would be to help both partners acquire a deeper understanding of Greek Orthodoxy's traditions and rituals.[88] These classes could be open to the general congregation, but be publicized as an "intermarriage" program. Such seminars might also be publicized as "A Couple's Night Out." Such an approach may prove more attractive to busy couples. If the seminar is shaped in such a way that balances learning and couple time, such a balance should function to draw some interest.

• If the church holds an annual festival, the festival committee might consider recruiting the time and talents of intermarried couples, with a concerted effort on reaching out to non-Orthodox partners in these marriages. There is also no reason to preclude non-Orthodox from assuming leadership positions during these community events.

• Because all communities have slightly different needs, the parish council should consider holding a brainstorming session to consider how it can utilize the time and talents of the non-Orthodox faithful who attend the church. Youth group leaders, Sunday School assistants, basic building problems and maintenance problems, as well as consultants on legal matters are a few ways that non-Orthodox can be brought closer to the center of community life.

• Continued respectful and collaborative contact after marriage with intermarried couples is also key to any effort to serve this group of faithful. All too often many of these couples wed in our churches and then drop out of sight. In an effort to reverse this tendency, communities might consider forming an intermarriage steering committee to assist the priest and parish council in its efforts to address this issue. Some suggested ideas and programs that these committees might consider implementing to begin reaching out more effectively to intermarried couples are listed below.

1. The first and fundamental rule of thumb should be to always provide intermarried couples with alternatives and information that is presented in such a manner that respects and honors their ability to choose what is best for them. Efforts at forcing or manipulating these couples into making decisions about religion for themselves and their families will simply be counterproductive. These tactics may either drive the non-Orthodox spouse away or alienate intermarried couples. Priests,

parents and lay workers should not push, manipulate and force non-Orthodox to convert.

2. Another effective outreach tool is the use of mentors. Briefly, this suggestion has been taken from a very successful national initiative called Marriage Savers[89] that has sought to address the high divorce rate in our country by linking engaged and distressed couples with happily married couples called mentors. While we are not necessarily talking about conflicted couples, by integrating this approach into our outreach efforts, new relationships are formed, and a safety net is constructed to assist this population as they seek to address their unique challenges. Mentors also provide clergy and lay leaders with an effective method to reach out to this population of faithful. As one focus group respondent stated, "Many of us know Sam. I'm not Greek, so when we first arrived he took me under his wing and showed me the ropes around here. I really appreciated that and it has gotten me thinking and praying about a lot of things pertaining to religion and the Greek Church." Of course, special care should be given when selecting these individuals and couples. They should be familiar with this resource and the resource entitled, *When You Intermarry*. They should also be involved in a healthy marriage – preferably an intermarriage – and have a respectful attitude for Greek Orthodox theology, traditions and customs.

3. Another option might be for local communities to produce a simple video that features intermarried couples who have successfully made their marriage work. Where this suggestion is impractical, pastors might simply consider selecting a few couples to speak about their experiences as successful intermarried couples in a panel discussion format that would be open to the congregation – especially intermarried couples.

4. Periodic marriage building seminars that are sensitive to intermarried couples' issues might be offered.[90] These seminars should focus attention on the meaning of marriage from an Orthodox and Christian perspective. They should seek to pro-

vide couples with effective skills that promote marital satisfaction and family stability. They could also include a component that discusses the unique challenges that intermarried couples and their families encounter. (See Chapters 7 – 11 for more information.)

5. Local churches might also consider forming an intermarried couples' support group. These groups would afford members the freedom to not only share their frustrations, but also hear how others are coping. In addition to reviewing the information in this resource and the resource for intermarried couples entitled, *When You Intermarry*, here are some other suggested topics for group discussion:

• Meeting your Individual Religious and Cultural Needs in an Intermarriage

• Meeting Your Religious Needs as a Couple

• Dealing with Intermarriage Parenting Challenges

• Coping with Extended Family Challenges

• I Don't Care What Day Your Mother Fasts – I Want Sausage on my Pizza!

• My Husband's a Methodist, His Mom is Methodist, and his Dad is Catholic, his Sister is Seventh Day Adventist: Steering Clear of Denominational Battles.

• What can we do as Intermarried Couples to Help the Local Greek Orthodox Church that we attend?

6. The local church could also consider offering more information on marriage and family issues in the church bulletin. Articles and personal reflections from the pastor's desk, positive personal reflections from parishioners, articles written by our theologians and other Orthodox professionals, as well as presentations from Orthodox family specialists is another way to help intermarried couples and families feel accepted.

7. If your community has a web site, you should also consider creating a link to the Interfaith Marriage Web site at www.interfaith.goarch.org. Including a Q & A from the chat rooms in the church bulletin might also be considered. There

are literally hundreds to choose from addressing a wide range of intermarriage challenges.

8. The use of English sends messages to intermarried couples that they are "accepted" and the use of too much Greek makes non-Greeks feel like "outsiders." As such, wherever possible, using more English in and outside of the services should be encouraged.

9. As a result of the increasingly secular society in which intermarried couples are embedded, the Church must continually strive to increase and improve its adult catechism classes. Results from the IRP strongly suggest that our faithful do not know their Orthodox faith. Results also indicate that many appear to understand that it is more important than ever that they learn more about their faith so that they can respond to the secular influences around them. Pastors and local church leaders must seek to find new and creative ways of making the many excellent resources that are currently available more accessible to their faithful. Church libraries and bookstores that feature the latest videos, books, tapes and CDs must be created and supported in a serious way at the local level. Quoting from one respondent, "In this information age that we live in our Orthodox message must be made available to our people, otherwise someone else's ideas will be."

10. Intermarried couples' decision to intermarry can sometimes create extended family problems, especially within Greek Orthodox family systems. Pastors and lay leaders should be sensitive to this and wherever possible seek to help extended Greek Orthodox family members understand and be more accepting to the couple's decision to intermarry. When pastors feel unqualified to do this type of work, they should be acquainted with a few trusted professionals that they can suggest. As one respondent stated, "The church must take a much more active role in its efforts to meet its marriages' and families' needs. Secular notions about marriage and divorce cannot simply be left unchallenged. We must do everything we can to

ensure that our marriages and families know that God can help them in their efforts to resolve domestic conflicts." (For more information see Chapters 7 – 11.)

Summary

Making an effort to address intermarried couples' unique needs can serve to benefit this growing population. This ministry will also ensure the Church's continued growth, as well as helping to further cultivate an evangelical attitude among all its faithful. The information in this chapter should be helpful in your efforts to begin reaching out to the intermarried couples and their families who choose to worship in the Greek Orthodox Church you serve.

Chapter Fourteen

The Value of Premarital Preparation For Intermarried Couples

Research indicates that premarital preparation has a positive impact on marriage. Outcome studies clearly indicate that premarital preparation can have a strong positive effect on the well-being of a couple's future children, couple communication, relationship quality and individual adjustment after marriage. Research also indicates that couples who have been through premarital preparation programs have a divorce rate that is considerably lower than that of the general public[91].

There are a number of different premarital preparation approaches that are being utilized across our Archdiocese. If you are currently using one of these approaches you are encouraged to continue. If you are not utilizing some form of premarital preparation, you are urged to contact your Diocese and, or the Archdiocese for guidance to assist you in implementing a premarital program. Together with the guidance you receive from the Diocese and, or Archdiocese, the following brief summaries of available premarital preparation materials may be helpful.

Kalellis, P. M. (1984). Preparing for Marriage. *Westfield, NJ: Ecumenical Publications*

This publication was produced by a marriage and family therapist who has a Greek Orthodox background and many years of experience working with couples. Its format is interactive and encourages partners to engage in conversation about important issues such as communication, in-laws, human sexuality and marriage from an Orthodox and Christian perspective. While this approach has many inherent strengths, I believe its most admirable quality is its use of mentor couples. Clergy who are understaffed and over committed should find this approach especially helpful, since the use of mentor couples make premarital preparation doable and highly effective. Along with the guidebook for couples, this approach includes an instructor's guide.

Mark, J. (1996). Preserve Them, O Lord. *Ben Lomond, CA: Conciliar Press.*

Preserve Them, O Lord is an interactive guide that has been written by an Orthodox priest, and is a useful resource for every Orthodox priest who is conducting premarital preparation. This book can also be utilized with couples who are conflicted and request counseling. This text is written in laymen's language and provides a concise, readable overview of the (a) Sacrament of Marriage, (b) our Orthodox theology on marriage, and (c) an Orthodox interpretation of numerous issues that may affect marriages. Its format is conducive to facilitating dialogue between couples, and should provide you with a convenient, structured format to help you assist couples who are preparing to receive the Sacrament of Marriage

Markey, B., Micheletto, M. (1996). Facilitating Open Couple Communication, Understanding and Study Facilitator Manual (FOCUS). *Omaha: Archdiocese of Omaha (402-551-9003).*

FOCUS is an empirically based 156 item instrument. It was developed originally by the Omaha Catholic Archdiocese but is now being utilized by numerous pastors and professionals across different faith communities. This instrument comes in three different versions: a Roman Catholic Edition, a Christian Non-Denominational Edition, and a Non-Denominational Edition. The Christian Non-Denominational Edition is a good supplement that will function to stimulate conversation between couples and enhance your efforts to prepare couples for marriage. This tool is especially effective in providing couples with insight from a psycho-educational, religious, and spiritual perspective. Unlike other psychometric tools, this instrument does not require extensive training or professional credentials before it can be utilized.

Crown Them with Glory and Honor: An Orthodox Christian Program of Life and Love for Engaged Couples and Couples About to be Engaged. *(1995). Greek Orthodox Diocese of Boston.*

This guidebook was produced by the St. Andrew Clergy Brotherhood of New England and is currently being used in the Boston Diocese. The guide provides an excellent overview of the Sacrament of Marriage, as well as an Orthodox perspective of marriage. It has also been written in a format that seeks to engage couples in meaningful conversation. Further information regarding this text can be obtained by contacting the Greek Orthodox Diocese of Boston.

In addition to the normal life cycle issues that intramarried couples face, intermarried couples must negotiate a host of additional challenges. When pastors make an effort to encourage engaged couples from different religious, cultural and racial backgrounds to take some time to consider how their religious and cultural differences can impact their lives after marriage, results from the IRP suggest that this can have a positive impact on couple communication, relationship quality, individual adjustment after marriage, and the well-being of the couple's future children.

How to use the Materials in This Section

The information provided in this chapter has not been written to replace the existing premarital preparation program you are currently using. You should, instead, view what follows as a supplement to whatever you are currently doing. These materials are organized around certain key questions that reflect the challenges that IRP respondents repeatedly described. You are encouraged to review the information that follows, and incorporate it when and where you deem it will be helpful[92].

In addition, you should be careful not to introduce these materials prematurely – especially during your first meeting. You should first seek to cultivate some trust and a working relationship with couples before broaching the subject of intermarriage. Once this is accomplished, then you can offer these materials with minimum resistance. Otherwise, many couples may view your efforts to introduce the subject of intermarriage with suspicion and question your motives.

One approach that might be helpful is to outline the premarital process at the end of the first meeting and present them with the materials you are planning to review. At that time you might consider presenting these couples with a copy of the resource entitled, *When You Intermarry,* and encourage them to begin reviewing the last chapter.

Expect Resistance From Some Couples

Despite your best efforts to avoid resistance, you might also remember that many of these couples will be anxious and nervous when first presenting themselves to "the priest" – especially when they meet with you alone. According to the IRP, here are a few observations to account for this uneasiness. Before meeting with you, many couples have grappled with numerous challenges in their efforts to appease individual, couple, and extended family concerns regarding their decision to intermarry. Having encountered some stressful challenges, many will also be concerned about other possible obstacles they may confront from "the priest."

Be forewarned, that while these couples stand to profit from the information that follows, some will view your intentions and motives to examine their religious and cultural differences with some reticence and suspicion. If this occurs, remember that these are normal reactions that people in our society tend to have when someone tries to offer unsolicited advice. So, please do not take these reactions personally and remember to preface your comments with the following information before introducing this subject.

• Assure the couple that you do not have any hidden agenda that will seek to either question or undermine their decision to intermarry.

• Tell them that you respect the non-Orthodox partner's decision to remain non-Orthodox.

• Let them also know that you are sharing this information as a way to help them prepare themselves to transition into married life as smoothly as possible.

Some Ways to use the Materials

This resource, along with the couple's resource entitled, *When You Intermarry,* are intended to be used together. Here are some recommended ways to use these materials. Once you acquaint yourself with these materials, you will likely find other ways to also use this information.

• Results from the IRP suggest that if a couple is inordinately uneasy with the prospects of engaging in conversation with the priest around intermarried issues, forcing the issue may merely compromise their relationship with the Orthodox Church. In these pastoral situations, you might simply present such couples with a copy of the resource for intermarried couples and respectfully urge them to review it privately. Once you have gained some trust, it may be that you can return and inquire about this subject.

• In other cases, you might choose to assign the last chapter of the intermarried couples' resource for homework and seek to engage the couple in some conversation during your next meeting. Subsequent meetings might also focus on addressing questions regarding the remainder of this resource.

• In some instances, you might choose to present the last chapter of the intermarried couples resource to a group of couples and encourage them to interact with each other about the contents[93]. In this case, it is best to find a way to facilitate an interactive learning experience, since couples will profit from each other's comments as much as they will from the information you present.

For those priests who plan to use these materials in a more interactive manner, a questionnaire has been designed to facilitate this process. Please turn to the end of the chapter for more information about this instrument. In addition, while there are many ways for you to utilize these materials, one way is to use the following protocol.

• At the end of your first meeting, present the intermarried couples resource to the couple or group and encourage them to review it.

• Ask them to complete the questionnaire at the end of this chapter for your next meeting. Encourage partners to complete the questions alone before they compare their answers. (This instrument is also located in chapter twelve in the couple's resource.)

• At your next meeting, ask them if they had any questions.

• Allow a dialogue to develop. While they are discussing the results, be available to offer information and suggestions. The following information should help you as you address their questions and concerns. You might also decide to refer them to the Interfaith Marriage Web site and Chat rooms at www.interfaith.goarch.org for additional information.

A Final Thought

I realize that many priests are too busy to provide a comprehensive overview of these materials. Furthermore, others may not want to enter into the kinds of intimate conversations that these materials require. If either of these observations apply to you, please do not feel compelled to do so. In most instances, you can acquaint yourself with these contents and present them to the couple. If you make yourself available for questions, this approach will generally suffice. Should you encounter a couple who has an inordinate number of couple challenges related to their religious and cultural differences and you are either unable or unqualified to address their issues and questions, you should be prepared to provide a referral.

Important Premarital Questions That Couples Should Consider

Question 1. Have we prayerfully discussed the pros and cons of entering into an inter-Christian marriage versus a single-church marriage?

Results from the IRP suggest that many couples get married in our churches without carefully considering the pros and cons of becoming an inter-Christian couple versus a single-church couple. The following reasons were repeatedly mentioned. And while all these reasons may not necessarily apply in each case, some of these factors will relate to each couple you meet who have different religious and cultural backgrounds.

• Respondents stated that they were committed to their faith tradition and viewed conversion as an unnecessary and/or unacceptable option.

• They did not want to hurt their parents' feelings and thus dismissed conversion as a serious option.

• They underestimated how their religious differences might affect them in the future, and felt that entering into an inter-Christian marriage would not pose any serious challenges.

• At the time when they married, one or both partners were nominally religious and did not consider religion a priority that needed to be addressed before marriage.

• Couples tended to believe that religion is a personal, private matter that concerns the individual and God.

• They were too busy preparing for a big wedding.

• They were concerned that too much conversation about their religious differences might have a toxic effect on their decision to get married.

• They believed that their religious and cultural differences could be resolved after marriage.

• One or both privately assumed that their partner might convert after marriage.

• Their own decision to enter into an inter-Christian marriage was influenced by the increasing number of individuals who are intermarrying in our society.

• They did not perceive any serious social stigma attached to intermarriage.

• Couples assumed that their mutual love would help them overcome all obstacles.

Results from the IRP also suggest that many couples have difficulty addressing this question in detail, and opt to ignore it. Conversely, results also suggest that a sizable number of participants believed that they might have profited from some type of premarital conversation related to this question, so long as this discussion could take place in a no pressure environment that would respect each individual's religious needs and sensitivities. Results further indicated that when pastors help partners consider this question faithfully and respectfully, more meaningful couple exchange tends to emerge.

Question 2. Have we prayerfully discussed the pros and cons of becoming an inter-Christian family versus a single-church family?

Results from the IRP suggest that many couples who get married in our churches have not carefully, honestly, and prayerfully considered the pros and cons of becoming an interchurch family versus a single-church family. Couples considering intermarriage should thus respectfully be urged to consider this question before marriage. You might also suggest that couples who neglect to address this issue before marriage will – according to the IRP – likely encounter this issue under more complex, difficult circumstances in the future after marriage. In addition, if after considering this issue carefully a given couple chooses to raise their children in an inter-Christian environment, their premarital discussions will have provided many of these couples with a less stressful beginning point from which to address this question effectively in the future when and if related challenges arise.

Results from the IRP also suggest that many couples assume certain issues regarding religion will fall into place when the children arrive. This approach is not a good way for intermarried couples to deal with their religious differences. The following example illustrates this point. (Along with this example, you may want to share examples from your own experiences to help couples consider this question.)

Frank (51) and Sophia (46) had been married for nearly 20 years. Their marriage was reasonably stable. However, lingering disagreements regarding their religious differences had created some marital contention, distance and family unhappiness. "We should have discussed this issue more before getting married, because we ended up creating some problems for us and our children," stated Sophia. "If I had it to do over again, I would not have intermarried," said Frank. Both were convinced that if they had spent some quality time discussing the value of becoming an interchurch couple verses a single-church couple many of their conflicts over religious issues might have been averted. They might have also opted to become a single-church family when the first child was old enough to enter Sunday School.

Once again, it is worth reiterating that while you may secretly desire couples to consider becoming an Orthodox family, your driving motivation when inviting couples to discuss this question should not be to proselytize the non-Orthodox partner. If you adopt this approach, most couples will discern what you are doing and your efforts will prove counterproductive. You should instead, assist the couple in carefully considering this issue so that they can arrive at a Christ-centered decision for themselves. Encouraging both individuals to engage in a conversation that is guided by Christian love, respect, and tolerance will prove invaluable to couples, especially couples who have previously failed to discuss this issue in detail. Such an approach will also prove more productive as you seek to help couples prayerfully discern the advantages of becoming a single-church couple.

Question 3. Have I been entirely honest with myself about entering an inter-Christian, inter-Church marriage?

Couples who participated in the IRP were asked to complete a 24-item questionnaire before they participated in their respective focus groups. One question in particular asked them to select the primary factor – from a listing of factors – that motivated them to get married. Ninety-nine percent chose the item labeled "love for my spouse." This high response rate is not unusual, since other research supports this finding.[94] In fact, the primary reason that couples in our society marry is related to their love for one another.

While "love for my spouse" is a good way to start a marriage, when and if you have the occasion to address this question, you might also remind couples of the wisdom behind the old saying, "what love conceals, time reveals." This is because love can cause engaged persons to ignore or disregard certain important personal needs. Results from the IRP suggest that some individuals love their partner so much that they are willing to ignore certain uncomfortable feelings and concerns connected to their religious differences before marriage. Results also suggest that some are so blinded by their love for their partner that they do not honestly consider their religious differences carefully. Unfortunately, after the honeymoon is over and somewhere into the first or second year of marriage, some of these individuals will begin to experience a combination of guilt and regrets because they failed to be honest with themselves and their spouse before marriage. Before marriage, these individuals may have felt a sense of discomfort about praying in separate churches, praying in their spouses' church, and raising their children in an inter-Christian and interchurch environment, but failed to be entirely honest with themselves before marriage. In one participant's words, "I never mentioned my concerns because we were in love, and I thought that love would help me accept some of the concessions my spouse was asking me to accept, but it didn't."

You might also remind couples that results from the IRP suggest that when individuals were honest with themselves regarding what they could and could not tolerate, this positively impacted their own adjustment after marriage as well as enhancing marital satisfaction. This was so because individuals and couples who were honest with themselves before marriage had fewer issues related to their religious differences to negotiate after marriage. Conversely, individuals who were not entirely honest with themselves struggled to find ways to address this omission after marriage. And while many of these types of omissions were successfully resolved after marriage, most of these participants repeatedly stated that some prayerful honesty with themselves before marriage might have served to make their adjustments after marriage less stressful.

Question 4. Have I been entirely honest with my spouse about entering an inter-Christian, inter-Church marriage?

With regard to this question, you might remind couples that it is important for them to be honest with one another regarding there religious preferences. Sharing some of the following information from the IRP should prove helpful to your efforts.

• Respondents indicated that a failure to be honest about this question could result in compromising marital trust and intimacy, as well as future marriage and family religious well-being.

• Respectful disclosure increased the likelihood that couples would grapple with issues related to religion collaboratively and respectfully rather than in an adversarial, controlling, manipulative manner.

• Respondents also stated that honest, respectful premarital conversations afforded them the opportunity to begin developing effective balancing strategies that helped them resolve future disagreements related to their religious and cultural differences.

• Participants also maintained that some honest dialogue during the premarital stage was usually all that was necessary to arrest most premarital concerns and help the couple transition more peacefully into married life.

Question 5. How do I meet my personal religious and spiritual needs in an intermarriage?

Results from the IRP suggest that most intermarried spouses were repeatedly challenged to find ways of meeting their religious and spiritual needs. For example, Greek Orthodox respondents stated that they struggled to find ways of (a) introducing icons in the home, (b) fasting, and (c) adequately explaining why it was important to them that they participate in many of the Orthodox Church's rites and rituals. Non-Orthodox respondents – especially those from a Protestant background – stated they struggled to (a) find ways of helping their Orthodox mate understand why "the sermon" was so important, (b) why they needed to hear certain familiar hymns, (c) why they felt uncomfortable with many of the unfamiliar rites, rules, and rituals in the Orthodox Church, and (d) why the use of inordinate amounts of Greek and certain ethnic differences impeded their efforts to pray and feel a part of the worshipping community when they attended their Greek Orthodox spouses' church. Respondents also indicated that when they failed to find ways of meeting their religious needs, their religious participation suffered. They also indicated that when this occurred, discussions with their mates about religion were generally characterized as contentious and, by extension, destabilizing their marriages.

While there are no simple recipes that couples can use to ensure their personal religious needs are met, couples involved in the IRP indicated that they found the following strategies useful in their efforts to address this need before marriage.

• Individual partners should clearly and respectfully articulate their religious needs to one another before marriage. This requires that one first be prayerfully honest with one's self and then respectfully share any concerns he or she may have with their future spouse before marriage.

• Partners should ask God for continued guidance. They should also understand that prayerful discussions will likely be needed of a similar nature after marriage, especially when and if one or both spouses sense that their religious needs are either being ignored or not met.

• Individuals should consider their partner's and children's religious needs. Otherwise they may be tempted to place an inordinate amount of importance on their needs to the detriment of their partner's and children's needs.

• After marriage, individual spouses should work toward increasing their knowledge of their own faith tradition so that they can help their partner acquire a deeper understanding and respect for their inherent religious needs. Individual spouses should also have a clear understanding of their partner's faith tradition.

• Both spouses should understand that disrespectful, manipulative, intolerant, controlling behavior of the type that seeks to dismiss and deprive one's partner from meeting his or her religious needs will negatively impact marital and family success and stability.

• When necessary, spouses and couples found it helpful to consult with their pastors or a professional couple's therapist for increased insight and direction. In many instances one or two meetings were sufficient to resolve couple disagreements.

Question 6. Is it necessary to be acquainted with my spouses' religious tradition?

Respondents involved in the IRP generally stressed the value of becoming reasonably well acquainted with both their own and their partner's religious needs and practices. They offered the following comments to reinforce this observation.

• When spouses understand why their partner desires to display icons, burn incense, light candles, have a family Bible, read and study scripture, pray spontaneously and without pre-authored prayers, this helped them develop a respectful attitude toward their partner's needs as well as their own.

• When spouses are more familiar with each faith tradition's rules, rituals, and rites, and how and why their own faith tradition differs, this can help to curb misunderstandings and hurt feelings that may be linked to inter-Christian couples' religious differences.

• Respondents stated that when they took the needed time to become familiar with their spouse's faith tradition, this helped them develop a keener understanding of their own religious needs and faith tradition. Such an effort also helped them develop a deeper faith in God.

• Respondents observed that when their pastors were amenable to helping them with this challenge, this positively impacted church attendance and commitment.

Question 7. Will we worship together or apart?

Results from the IRP clearly indicate that when couples fail to spend quality time discussing this question before marriage, this question will invariably challenge them after marriage.

Results also indicate that most inter-Christian couples value couple and family worship. However, it is not always easy for them to worship together. One of the main obstacles precluding couple and family worship is related to both partners' commitment to their faith tradition. If both spouses have equally strong commitments to their faith tradition, it will be somewhat difficult for them to make the needed adjustments so that they will be able to worship together. When one spouse has a strong commitment, and the other has a weak commitment, such couples have an easier time determining if they will worship apart or together. In instances where both partners have equally low levels of religiosity, these couples will likely experience the least number of challenges. Because couples encounter different challenges by virtue of their different levels of religious commitment, the following suggested responses to this question will take this into account.

When Both Spouses Have High Religious Commitment

• In the case where both spouses have an equally strong commitment to their faith tradition, these couples appear to have an especially difficult time finding ways of meeting each individual's needs as well as their need and desire to worship together. In some cases, these couples eventually succeed in striking a balance between individual needs, couple and family needs. These couples will generally end up making adjustments that serve to meet both individual and couple/family needs, but not without some compromise and regrets. For example, in the case of a Roman Catholic and Orthodox couple, the Catholic spouse may attend a Saturday evening Mass to meet his or her personal religious needs and then accompany his or her spouse/family to divine liturgy on Sunday morning. These spouses may either remain intermarried or eventually become a single-churchcouple and family. This is especially true when parents decease or when the children are old enough to attend Sunday School.

• When the children are finally launched from the home, some of these couples may end up worshipping in separate churches. This happens because the non-Orthodox partner has made the concession to worship in the partner's church, but has been unsuccessful in meeting his or her religious needs in the partner's faith community. This seems to occur with more frequency if the couple has been unsuccessful in making peace with their religious differences.

• In other instances, when both spouses have equally strong commitments to their faith tradition, some never succeed in worshiping together. There are numerous reasons why this is the case. Some are: spouses do not feel comfortable worshiping in their partner's church; spouses desire to receive the sacraments regularly; spouses do not have the time to attend two church services regularly.

• If inter-church spouses with equally strong religious commitments determine to worship together, you should respectfully try to make these couples cognizant of the following caveats. The spouse who has made concessions will likely feel somewhat short-changed. In addition, the other partner will feel somewhat guilty because he or she is aware of these concessions. Both spouses are also likely to feel somewhat empty and saddened because they realize that their religious differences prevent them from cultivating intimacy and oneness in this dimension of their lives.

• After some frustrations, most couples use their Christian Faith to help them circumvent their religious differences and disappointments. God's grace helps them make the needed adjustments to protect marital and family stability and well-being and meet their individual religious needs.

Unequal Religious Commitment

• When inter-Christian couples with unequal religious commitments wed, particularly when one partner has a strong religious commitment and the other has a weak religious commitment, many of these couples often have an easier time addressing this question – especially when some premarital conversation has occurred. Results from the IRP suggest that the spouse with the nominal faith (so long as he or she does not have high ethnic attachments) will generally attend their spouse's church and defer to their "religious" spouse when it comes to the family's religious needs. This spouse may also consider embracing their partner's faith tradition.

• While the number of challenges will usually be less among these types of couples, they will not be immune to certain challenges. For example, with the exception of Christmas, Easter or an occasional baptism or wedding, in many of these marriages, the rule of thumb is that the spouse with the stronger religious commitment will generally attend church services alone. This also means that an important part of one spouse's life will never be shared on an intimate level with the nominal believer.

• These spouses may also experience some lingering disagreements with regards to the value of religion. This could affect marital and family stability. The spouse with the strong commitment may end up becoming somewhat defensive and confrontational as a result of his or her partner's indifference to religion.

• In other instances, the spouse with the weaker commitment might be the one to become defensive and confrontational, while the spouse with the strong faith might become discouraged and saddened by his or her partner's negative reactions toward religion. In either of these two cases, pastors can be very helpful to couples who are struggling with these religious differences.

• When inter-Christian spouses with unequal religious commitments choose to marry they should also be aware of the following caveats. Failure to address their unequal religious commitments before marriage can produce marital and family conflict when the issue of couple worship is eventually addressed. Discussions regarding religious worship should seek to respectfully take each spouse's feelings and thoughts into consideration. Reaching a mutually agreeable understanding around this can positively impact individual, couple and family well-being.

Spouses With Equally Low Levels of Religiosity

• These couples will likely experience the fewest number of individual and couple challenges. However, they are not entirely immune to challenges, since extended family members often exert minimal pressures on their lives. These couples may or may not respond to these extended family pressures. If they do, the interactions may likely be contentious in nature. These negative interactions may also prompt some parents to consult you for guidance. For the most part, those couples who request the Sacrament of Marriage for reasons related to extended family needs are not necessarily religiously or spiritually motivated.

• While it is sometimes somewhat tempting to do the minimum amount of premarital preparation with these couples, please keep in mind that you are sowing seeds that may eventually germinate. So, try not to cut too many corners when preparing these couples for marriage. In many instances, you may give one or both partners something to think about that could result in helping them discern the value of a religious lifestyle. This may be especially the case when the children arrive.

Question 8. Have we discussed our religious financial commitments?

Disagreements stemming over the way couples manage their finances are not uncommon. When couples fail to strike a mutually satisfying understanding regarding their finances, this can create serious marital conflict. It is thus important that intermarried couples discuss the manner in which they will pledge. Pastors can advise inter-Church couples to consider questions similar to those listed below. Moreover, a failure to do so may result in creating hurt feelings and unexpected marital disagreements.

- Can we afford to pledge to two churches?
- How will we determine what amounts to pledge to both churches?
- If we only pledge to my church, how will that affect my partner?
- If we don't pledge to my church, how will that affect me?

Question 9. How much of a Greek Orthodox home will we have?

Greek Orthodoxy is not only practiced on Sunday mornings, but is a lifestyle that affects each moment of a person's life. According to results from the IRP, couples who failed to consider this question repeatedly stated that some mutual agreement before marriage would have reduced marital stress. Pastors should encourage their faithful to carefully consider the above question together with similar collateral questions listed below.

- Where will the icons go in our inter-Christian home?

• How will my non-Orthodox partner react to my burning incense?
• What will our diet look like around the Orthodox Church's fasting periods?
• How will we pray together as a couple at home?

Question 10. In which partner's faith tradition will the children be baptized?

The following story illustrates some of the problems that intermarried couples encounter when they fail to discuss the issue of baptism before the first child arrives. While this example may contain challenges that are more intense than most couples may encounter, the circumstances and related challenges this couple encounters are not entirely unusual.

Sam (27) and Emily (28) had been married for three years. Emily is Roman Catholic and Sam is Greek Orthodox. Before their marriage, Sam assumed that the couple's children would be baptized Greek Orthodox, since they were married in the Greek Orthodox Church. However, he never shared this assumption with Emily before marriage. Emily also assumed that the couple would discuss this issue before making any decisions.

As a result of their busy schedule, this couple never broached this issue until three months after the birth of their first child when Sam suggested that they make an appointment with his priest to have their child baptized. This suggestion surprised and hurt Emily, and the couple proceeded to have a serious disagreement that caused them to postpone their child's baptism.

Sam eventually got Emily to give in, and their baby was baptized. However, the baptism was not, a joyous event. Throughout the process Emily did not understand the symbolism, she felt the priest treated her deferentially, she resented her in-laws efforts to disregard her ethnic background and turn the reception into "a Greek affair," and she was especially upset at how unsympathetic Sam was to her needs. Moreover, this resentment lingered even after the baptism, and caused additional disagreements to surface regarding their child's religious and spiritual development.

While most baptisms are not this unsettling, most pastors who have spent any time in the ministry know that scenarios like this one are not uncommon. Pastors do many couples a great favor when they encourage them to prayerfully consider this question and other related questions concerning their future children's religious and spiritual development.

- Will I be upset if my children were baptized in my spouse's church?
- Will my marriage be negatively impacted if I insist that we baptize our children in my faith tradition?
- Will my parents be upset if our children are baptized in my spouse's church?
- Will my in-laws be upset if we baptize our children in my faith tradition?

Question 11. How will the children develop their religious identity?

Results from the IRP clearly indicate that inter-Christian and inter-Church spouses and parents frequently espouse a respect and tolerance for difference. Consequently, results from the IRP suggest that intermarried parents seek to consciously expose their children to numerous religious and cultural traditions, including both parents' religious and cultural traditions.

Conversely, results suggest that most parents deliberately seek to inculcate them in one faith tradition. Furthermore, parents who made this choice reported that this decision turned out to be in the best interest of their children's religious and spiritual development. Parents who remained conflicted over this issue, and chose to raise their children in both churches, regretted this decision for the following reasons:

- While it was not necessarily detrimental to raise their children to have respect for other religious traditions, and to occasionally bring them to the other spouse's church, children must be raised in one faith tradition. Just as parental agreement is key in other dimensions of their children's development, it is equally important to their children's religious well-being. Parents who are conflicted over their religious differences negatively impact their children's religious development.

• Parents' mutual decision to raise their children in one church ended up providing them with the needed consistency and structure that they required to bond to a faith tradition, and develop a religious identity.

Respondents strongly maintained that parents should not choose to raise some of their children in one parent's faith tradition and others in the other parent's faith tradition. In these instances, respondents stated that this served to compromise their children and family's religious well-being. They further stated that even though such an approach may have made each partner feel better, it served to send mixed messages to their children that ultimately diluted the parents' efforts to provide needed consistency and structure, and impeded their children's efforts to bond with a faith tradition and develop a religious identity.

On the strength of this information, you should advise engaged persons contemplating an intermarriage to discuss this question carefully before marriage and come to some tentative mutually agreeable decisions. You might also suggest that a failure to do so may negatively impact their future children's religious and spiritual growth.

Question 12. How do we deal with our future children's questions regarding our intermarriage?

As children mature, they begin to ask their parents questions in an effort to piece their physical and social worlds together. Furthermore, some of these questions will inevitably be related to religious matters. Along with the questions that single-churchparents contend with regarding religion, intermarried parents must contend with questions that are related to their religious differences. Sooner or later, little Tommy or Sophia will detect that Daddy does not receive communion with the rest of the family, or Mommy does not do the sign of the Cross, or Daddy goes to a different church on Sunday mornings. When this occurs, questions invariably follow.

Before this time arrives, and it will arrive sooner then most engaged couples think, couples contemplating intermarriage should be advised to begin considering how they will address these questions. The following information from the IRP should function to help pastors in their efforts to assist couples to prepare themselves for these inevitable questions.

According to the results from the IRP, many parents stated that these questions were particularly difficult for them to answer. One factor that accounts for this is that most parents are invested in protecting and nurturing their children's developing religious identity. These parents did not want to say anything that might compromise their children's efforts to bond with the faith tradition in which they were being raised. Another factor was connected to parents' desire for their children to develop a respect for both parents' religious tradition, as well as a respect and tolerance for other religious traditions. And finally, one last complicating factor was linked to their determination that they would not allow their religious differences to divide the members of their family and compromise marital and family stability.

Given these varied and seemingly irreconcilable concerns, participants involved in the IRP used one or more of the following strategies to help them answer their children's religious questions – especially as they were related to their parents' religious differences.

- Participants stated that parents should try not to feel threatened by questions related to their religious differences. They further observed that in most cases children are simply asking questions out of curiosity because they have a need to make sense of their world. When intermarried parents remember this, they will be less inclined to ignore these questions or answer defensively, and will likely provide the meaningful information that their children require.

• They also stated that intermarried parents should have a mutual understanding regarding their children's religious development, otherwise they will likely fail to articulate meaningful answers to their children. If children are told that they should have respect for other people's faith tradition, but they observe their parents in conflict over religion, the result will undermine their efforts to address their children's concerns. Children will learn what parents model for them.

• In addition, participants observed that meaningful answers do not just simply appear out of thin air, but are dependent on a parent's knowledge of their faith tradition and their partner's faith tradition. Otherwise their responses may fail to be balanced and respectful. This point presupposes that parents either know their faith or seek to educate themselves about their faith tradition.

• Participants also observed that when answering their children's questions, they must seek to stress what both parents' faith traditions have in common and minimize their differences. Specifically, they stated that parents should remind their children that all members of the family are Christians and that they all worship the same God. Respondents also suggested that they should remind their children that just as Mom and Dad are proud of their own religious faith tradition and respect each other's faith traditions, they also should be proud of their faith tradition and be respectful of other faith traditions.

• Participants also stated that parents should consciously avoid speaking in pejorative terms about other religious and cultural traditions, and constantly remind their children that God made and loves all people equally.

Question 13. How do we honor and respect our own parents in our efforts to raise our children?

Grandparents desire that their grandchildren be exposed to their religious and cultural traditions. Moreover, in some instances they will employ invasive, manipulative means to ensure that this occurs. For example, they may apply pressure in an effort to get the couple to baptize and raise their grandchildren in their church. They may also seek to apply pressure on their adult child in an effort to undermine the couple's decisions regarding their grandchildren. For example, consider the following brief illustration.

John (27) and Fran (28) have been married for two years. They have just received the news that they are expecting their first child. John proceeds to call his parents. They congratulate him and then remind him that they are expecting him to baptize the child in the Greek Orthodox Church. Wishing to preserve the warmth of the moment, John pretends to agree by not responding to his parent's demands.

Later, Fran asks about his conversation with his parents. Rather than sharing what his parents said, John reacts with some annoyance and gruffly states "Nothing." The issue is dropped, but not forgotten. In the next few months that follow John's parents remind him numerous times of "his promise." Of course, John feels unsettled by these constant reminders, and in an effort to stop their hounding eventually says, "I know, I know, so stop reminding, me – okay?"

All is forgotten for a few more months, until the day Fran comes home from a visit with John's parents. Fuming with anger, she asks, "So, did you tell your parents that our baby will be baptized in the Greek Church without consulting me?" John does not answer, but his face gives his secret away. "How could you, John? " she states. She then becomes very angry and upset.

Fortunately, this couple was able to reconcile their differences, but not before John confronted his parents and informed them that while he loved them both, this was between him and his wife. He further stated that if they did not choose to baptize their child in the Greek Orthodox Church, it was not because they did not love or respect them, but because it was the best thing for their growing family. This does not sit well with John's parents. However, as a result of the couple holding firm to this position, John's parents eventually realized that they must withdraw their demands and try and think of what is best for their son's family.

According to participants in the IRP, engaged inter-Christian couples should be aware that they may encounter unwanted extended family pressures in their efforts to raise their children. As such, you should seek to remind couples of the indispensable value of the following information in their efforts to deal with unwanted extended family pressures after marriage.

- Couples reported that family of origin allegiances verses nuclear family allegiances can potentially create distance between spouses. Individual spouses can be torn between their family of origin's religious and cultural allegiances and their spouse's religious preferences and family needs. These diametrically opposing familial pulls can inhibit a couple's efforts to make decisions about religious and cultural matters that concern their family, as well as create some distance in their marriage. This is especially the case during the first few years of a marriage.
- Couples must learn how to draw clear boundaries between their nuclear family and their extended families with regards to religion and culture. They must learn to resolve their religious differences apart from their extended families, and avoid permitting extended family biases to contaminate their decisions about their children's religious development. Drawing clear, healthy boundaries between themselves and both families of origin is important in their efforts to meet their children's religious needs.

Question 14. Am I aware of the Orthodox Church's rules pertaining to intermarried couples?

Couples who participated in the intermarriage research process repeatedly indicated that they were reasonably ignorant "of how the Orthodox Church's rules applied to intermarried couples." Furthermore, they also indicated that it would have been helpful to them if at some juncture during the premarital preparation process "this information had been presented to them." Since many of these spouses want this information, at some point you should take some time to review the pastoral directives listed in this resource in Chapter 12.

In addition, when reviewing these directives with inter-church engaged persons, pastors should avoid taking a dogmatic approach, and assume a collaborative non-judgmental posture that is intended to educate these couples. By assuming this pastoral approach, the couple will have received some needed and desired information that will help them in the future, as well as the needed space to understand the Orthodox Church's rules as they apply to intermarried couples.

Question 15. Do I know why my non-Orthodox in-laws cannot receive the sacraments in the Greek Orthodox Church?

Engaged persons are especially interested in putting their best foot forward in their efforts to develop a positive relationship with their future in-laws. However, one eventuality that can compromise this effort may be linked to non-Orthodox family members' reactions to the Greek Orthodox Church's rules regarding sacramental participation. While most engaged persons will likely not encounter any major difficulties with in-laws regarding this issue, they may profit from considering the following materials in the event that such problems emerge.

Participants involved in IRP observed that our church's religious and ethnic exclusivity frequently served to create tension between them and the non-Orthodox partner's extended family. In these cases, participants noted that non-Orthodox extended family members described feeling especially disconcerted with the Orthodox Church's rules regarding their participation in the sacraments. Several participants also described hurt feelings that non-Orthodox extended family members felt when they were informed they could not function as a sponsor or godparent. In an effort to avert some of these hurt feelings, participants observed that the following strategies tended to be helpful in minimizing tension between non-Orthodox extended family members and the inter-church couple.

- The Greek Orthodox partner must be sufficiently knowledgeable of his or her faith tradition so as to address their partners and extended family's questions regarding non-Orthodox participation in the Greek Orthodox Church.
- Both partners should present a unified front when addressing extended family questions. They should also address them in a non-confrontational, Christian, and respectful manner.
- The non-Orthodox spouse should take the lead in trying to explain the Orthodox Church's position, and the Orthodox partner should assume a consultant's role. Under no circumstances should the Greek Orthodox partner assume the lead role when the situation is potentially explosive.
- Inter-church couples should expect that some non-Orthodox extended family members may require time to digest and accept the Orthodox Church's rules, and in some instances may never entirely agree. When non-Orthodox family members do not agree, the couple should try to cultivate a "let's agree to disagree" attitude, and avoid arguing.
- Intermarried couples should try to view non-Orthodox extended family members' confusion about the Orthodox Church's rules as opportunities for family growth and religious growth.

Question 16. Have we discussed how we will respect each other's cultural traditions and preferences?

Many intermarried couples who present themselves to the pastor requesting the Sacrament of Marriage will both have a predominantly Americanized perspective with very attenuated ethnic attachments, while a sizeable number of these individuals will also come from different ethnic traditions and have moderate to high ethnic attachments. As a result, this question may or may not necessarily apply to each intermarried couple that you will work with during the premarital preparation process. Furthermore, in cases where only one partner has a strong connection to their ethnic background, these potential unions may have slightly different challenges than those couples where both spouses have a distinct ethnic connection.

Pastors preparing intercultural couples are thus advised to encourage these couples to examine how their ethnic differences might impact individual adjustment and marital quality. Since ethnic differences can be a potentially destabilizing force – especially during the first few years in these marriages – the following observations from the IRP together with your own examples may help couples begin to address this question.

• Non-Greek Orthodox respondents frequently stated that they experienced low to moderate levels of culture shock during the first few years of marriage. In these cases, they indicated that they found Greek American families to be generally more emotionally expressive and enmeshed than their own families of origin. While they learned to admire and appreciate this dimension of Greek American extended family life, it took them some time to develop a comfort level with these and other cultural and ethnic differences.

• In other instances, participants indicated that they felt moderately challenged to find ways of blending two different ethnic cooking traditions together. In these instances, some non-Greek Orthodox participants who had come from families that cooked decidedly American cuisine indicated that they had some difficulty adjusting to the large amounts of garlic and oregano that Greeks tended to use in their cooking. Couples also stated that extended family expectations around Christmas and Easter also challenged them. Many non-Greek spouses stated that Lenten and Easter traditions were especially perplexing to them. Non-Greeks also reacted to other Greek traditions such as the naming of the first-born child after the Greek partner's parents.

• As a result, information from the IRP indicates that some premarital discussion focusing around ethnic and cultural differences seemed somewhat valuable to persons from (a) different ethnic backgrounds, and (b) to couples with different degrees of ethnic attachment. Couples who put aside time to discuss their cultural differences felt more comfortable about these differences and more assured that their differences would be respected after marriage. These couples also indicated that continued conversation after marriage was equally important to them in their efforts to profit from their ethnic differences. To facilitate couples' efforts to discuss their ethnic and cultural differences, you might suggest they consider the following list of questions.

• Have we talked about the food and drink we prefer?

• Can I live with someone who is inclined to support Turkey rather than Greece?

• Have I let my partner know how much of a Greek home I want?

• Do I know how many ethnic customs are acceptable to my partner?

• Do I know how much of a non-Greek home my partner wants?

• Have I thought about how much of a non-Greek home is acceptable to me?

• Have we discussed how we will raise our children to be respectful to both spouses' ethnic backgrounds?

Question 17. Is it necessary to be acquainted with my future spouse's ethnic and cultural background?

According to results from the IRP, an answer to this question depends on how important each individual spouse's cultural and ethnic tradition is. Obviously, if culture and ethnicity is of little or no importance to both future partners, then it stands to reason that this concern is essentially moot. If one or both spouses' ethnic backgrounds are moderately to highly valued, then some efforts to understand and respect one or both spouses respective ethnic backgrounds will prove profitable in reducing any potentially destabilizing affects that might occur from spouses' ethnic differences. The following example, together with your own experiences may help you get couples to consider this question in more detail.

Ann (24) and Gus (28) had been married for three years. Gus considered his Greek background important, and persisted in trying to incorporate Greek traditions into his married life. Gus was not, however, as keenly interested in understanding Ann's Irish background, and frequently spoke in disparaging terms about the Irish. One day, after a particularly long tirade about the Irish, Ann could no longer remain quiet, and let Gus knows in no uncertain terms. Fortunately, Gus listened to his wife, and apologized saying, "I honestly didn't know your Irish background meant anything to you, because you never talk about it. I'm sorry, it won't happen again."

Assessing your Readiness to Intermarry

Have individual spouses read each statement and circle **Y** for "yes" and **N** for "no."

1. Have we prayerfully discussed the pros and cons of intermarriage? **Y** **N**

____

2. Have we prayerfully discussed the pros and cons of becoming a single-church family? **Y** **N**

____

3. Have I been entirely honest with *myself* about entering an inter-church, inter-Christian marriage? **Y** **N**

____

4. Have I been entirely honest with *my spouse* about entering an inter-church, inter-Christian marriage? **Y** **N**

____

5. Have we discussed how each of us will meet our personal religious and spiritual needs in an inter-Christian marriage? **Y** **N**

____

6. Is it necessary to be acquainted with my *spouse's* religious tradition? **Y** **N**

____

7. Have we decided whether we will worship together or apart? **Y** **N**

____

8. Have we discussed our religious financial commitments?
Y **N**

____

9. Can we afford to pledge to two churches?
Y **N**

____

10. Have we determined what amounts we will pledge to our respective churches? **Y** **N**

____

11. If we only pledge to my church, will that affect my partner? **Y** **N**

____

12. If we don't pledge to my church, will that affect me?
Y **N**

____

13. Is it important for us to consider how much of a Greek Orthodox home we will have? **Y** **N**

____

14. Have we talked about where the icons will go in our home? **Y** **N**

____

15. Do I know how my non-Orthodox partner will react when I burn incense? **Y** **N**

____

16. Have we talked about what our diet will look like around the Orthodox Church's fasting periods?
Y **N**

____

17. Have we talked about how we will pray together as a couple in our home? **Y** **N**

____

18. Have we talked about where our future children will be baptized? **Y** **N**

____

19. Will I be upset if our children are baptized in my spouse's church? **Y** **N**

____

20. Will my marriage be negatively impacted if I insist that we baptize and raise our children in my faith tradition? **Y** **N**

____

21. Will my parents be upset if our children are baptized in my spouse's church? **Y** **N**

____

22. Will my in-laws be upset if we baptize our children in my faith tradition? **Y** **N**

____

23. Have we talked about how our children will develop their religious identity? **Y** **N**

____

24. Have we talked about how we will deal with our future children's questions regarding our inter-Christian marriage? **Y** **N**

____

25. Does honoring and respecting our parents mean that we should acquiesce to their demands when it comes to making decisions about our children's religious and spiritual development?

Y N

____

26. Am I aware of the Orthodox Church's rules pertaining to intermarried couples? **Y N**

____

27. Are we aware of the Orthodox Church's rules?

Y N

____

28. Do I know why my non-Orthodox in-laws cannot receive the sacraments in the Greek Orthodox Church?

Y N

____

29. Should my future in-laws want information about non-Orthodox participation in the Orthodox Church's sacraments, have we discussed how we will explain the Orthodox Church's position?

Y N

____

30. Have we discussed how we will respect each other's cultural traditions and preferences?

Y N

____

31. Is it necessary to be acquainted with my future spouse's ethnic/cultural background?

Y N

____

Scoring. Spouses should give themselves one point for each "yes" answer. They should then add and combine their scores.

If a couple scores 40 or better, let them know that they are well on the way toward finding some respectful, holy agreement regarding their religious and cultural differences. You should also encourage these couples to review their answers together so that they can consider where their points of disagreement might exist. Offering your assistance as they discuss their points of disagreements should also help them.

If a couple scores less than 40, you might recommend that they acquire a copy of the intermarried couple's resource for present and future reference. You might also indicate that while their low score does not indicate that they will experience future marital and family instability, it does suggest that they could benefit from some additional prayerful discussion. Your assistance may prove invaluable in this instance. As such, I would not hesitate to offer your time. Your efforts will likely prove invaluable to such couples while affording them another good way to develop a bond with you and the Greek Orthodox Church.

Notes

[1] For additional information about postmodernism, consult the following reference: Kuhn, T. (1970). *The structure of scientific revolutions*. Chicago: University of Chicago Press.
[2] Waite, L. J. & Gallagher, M. (2000). *The case for marriage: Why married people are happier, healthier, and better off financially*. New York: Doubleday.
[3] Chrysostom, J. (1997). *St. John Chrysostom: On marriage and family life* (C. P. Roth & D. Anderson, Trans.). Crestwood, NY: St. Vladimir's Seminary Press.
[4] For additional information concerning marriage from an Orthodox perspective, consider consulting the following few resources: Constantelos, D. (1975). *Marriage sexuality and celibacy: A Greek Orthodox perspective*. Minneapolis, MN: Light and Life Publishing Company. Evdokimov, P. (1985). *The sacrament of love*. Crestwood, NY: St. Vladimir's Seminary Press. Mack, J. (1996). *Preserve them O Lord*. Ben Lomond, CA: Conciliar Press. Meyendorff, J. (1975). *Marriage: An Orthodox perspective*. Crestwood, NY: St. Vladimir's Seminary Press.
[5] Since the overwhelming majority of intermarried couples belonging to our churches are inter-Christian and intercultural, this guidebook has been written for these types of couples. While much of the information in this guidebook may apply to other types of intermarried couples, the specific challenges facing other types of intermarriages, such as interreligious marriages, will not be addressed in this guidebook. This resource will seek to assist inter-Christian couples who have chosen to attend a Greek Orthodox Church.
[6] Stephanopoulos, N. (Ed.). (2001). *Greek Orthodox Archdiocese of America yearbook 2001*. New York: Greek Orthodox Archdiocese of America.
[7] Statistics from the Chicago Diocese indicate that from 1/90 through 8/98 (41%) of all marriages conducted in this diocese were Orthodox/Catholic marriages, while (39%) were Orthodox/Orthodox marriages.

[8] For more information, please consult the following two references: Chimbos, P. (1999). Interethnic marriages and prospects for ethnic group survival: The case of Greek Canadian. In S. J. Tremberis, H. J. Psomiades & A. Karpathakis (Eds.), *Greek American families: Traditions and transformations*. New York, NY: Pella Publishing Company. Counelis, J. S. (1989). Greek Orthodox Church statistics of the United States, 1949-1989: Some ecclesial and social patterns. *Journal of the Hellenic Diaspora*, 16, 129-159.

[9] If the reader is interested in more details regarding what conversations have transpired prior to the writing of this manual, the following reference should prove instructive: Vrame, A.C. (Ed.). (1997). *InterMarriage: Orthodox perspectives*. Brookline, MA: Holy Cross Orthodox Press.

[10] Evdokimov, P. (1985). *The sacrament of love*. Crestwood, NY: St. Vladimir's Seminary Press.

[11] Joanides, C. (2002). *When you intermarry: A resource for inter-Christian, intercultural couples, parents and families*. Brookline, MA: Greek Orthodox Archdiocese of America. Throughout the remainder of this book, I will generally refer to this manual as the resource for intermarried couples.

[12] This resource was primarily produced for clergy and lay workers. To that end, lay workers with professional backgrounds such as licensed psychotherapists and educators will find its contents useful. Other paraprofessionals such as youth workers, lay assistants and parish council members can also benefit from this information.

[13] Counelis, J. S. (1989). Greek Orthodox Church Statistics of the United States, 1949-1989: Some ecclesial and social patterns. *Journal of the Hellenic Diaspora*, 16, 129-159.

[14] Stephanopoulos, N. (Ed.). (2001). *Greek Orthodox Archdiocese of America yearbook 2001*. New York: Greek Orthodox Archdiocese of America.

[15] Harakas, S. (1997). Emerging ecumenical families. In A. C. Vrame (Ed.) *InterMarriage: Orthodox perspectives*. Brookline, MA: Holy Cross Orthodox Press.

[16] Tsemberis, S. J. (1999). Greek American families: Immigration, acculturation, and psychological well-being. In S. J. Tremberis, H. J.

Psomiades & A. Karpathakis (Eds.), *Greek American families: Traditions and transformations*. New York, NY: Pella Publishing Company.
[17] Vrame, A. C. (Ed.). (1997). *Interfaith marriage: Orthodox perspectives*. Brookline, MA: Holy Cross Orthodox Press.
[18] Gottman, J. M. (1994). *What predicts divorce?* Hillsdale, New Jersey: Lawrence Erlbaum Associates, Publishers.
[19] Waite, L. J. & Gallagher, M. (2000). *The case for marriage: Why married people are happier, healthier, and better off financially*. New York: Doubleday.
[20] Waite, L. J. & Gallagher, M. (2000). *The case for marriage: Why married people are happier, healthier, and better off financially*. New York: Doubleday.
[21] Harakas, S. (1997). Emerging ecumenical families. In A. C. Vrame (Ed.) *InterMarriage: Orthodox perspectives*. Brookline, MA: Holy Cross Orthodox Press.
[22] Lorant, S. & Wingenbach, G. (1996). *Proceedings from 33rd Clergy-Laity Congress: Report of the committee on interchurch and interfaith marriages*. New York: NY.
[23] For further information please consult Fr. Charles Joanides, Ph.D., LMFT at the following address: Greek Orthodox Archdiocese of America, 8-10 East 79th Street, New York, NY 10021.
[24] Roof, W. C. (1999). *Spiritual marketplace: Baby boomers and the remaking of American religion*. Princeton, New Jersey: Princeton University Press.
[25] Joanides, C. (2002). *When you intermarry: A resource for inter-Christian, intercultural couples, parents and families*. New York, NY: Greek Orthodox Archdiocese of America.
[26] Georgakas, D. (1999). The America beyond Ellis Island. In S. J. Tremberis, H. J. Psomiadis & A. Karpathakis. *Greek American families: Traditions and transformations*. New York: Pella Inc.
[27] Since the overwhelming majority of intermarried couples belonging to our churches are inter-Christian and intercultural, this guidebook has been written for these types of couples. While much of the information in this guidebook may apply to other types of intermarried couples, the specific challenges facing other types of intermarriages, such as interreligious marriages, will not be addressed in this guidebook. This resource will seek to assist clergy and lay leaders in their efforts to minister to inter-Christian couples who have chosen to attend a Greek Orthodox Church. My hope is that future research will also address the pastoral needs of inter-religious couples.

[28] As an example of this assertion, consider the following excellent resource: Vrame, A. C. (Ed.). (1997). *InterMarriage: Orthodox perspectives*. Brookline, MA: Holy Cross Orthodox Press. This resource contains a wealth of information regarding intermarriage, but nothing from the perspective of intermarried couples.
[29] Morgan, D. L. (1998). *Planning focus groups: Focus group kit 2*. Thousand Oaks, CA: Sage Publications.
[30] This site served to strengthen the credibility of this research, and can be accessed at www.interfaith.goarch.org.
[31] Denzin, N. K. & Lincoln, Y. S. (1994). *Handbook of qualitative research*. Thousand Oaks, CA: Sage.
[32] A copy of this questionnaire can be obtained by contacting Fr. Charles Joanides.
[33] A listing of all questions utilized can be obtained by contacting Fr. Charles Joanides.
[34] The following references can be consulted for information pertaining to grounded theory. Glazer, B. G. & Strauss, A. L. (1965). *The discovery of grounded theory: Strategies for qualitative research*. New York: Aldine Publishing Co. Glazer, B. G. & Strauss, A. L. (1967). *The discovery of grounded theory: Strategies for qualitative research*. New York: Aldine Publishing Co. Strauss, A. & Corbin, J. (1990). *Basics of qualitative research: Grounded theory procedures and techniques*. Newbury Park, CA: Sage.
[35] The following reference can be consulted for more information about naturalistic inquiry: Lincoln, Y. & Guba, E. (1985). *Naturalistic inquiry*. Newbury Park: Sage.
[36] This information can also be found in the couple's resource entitled, *When you intermarry: A Resource for inter-Christian, intercultural couples, parents and families*. It is offered in this manual to ensure that clergy and lay workers are exposed to this important material.
[37] This information appears in the couple's resource entitled, *When you intermarry: A Resource for inter-Christian, intercultural couples, parents and families*. It is offered in this manual to ensure that clergy and lay leaders review these important materials.
[38] Lawler, M. G., Markey, B., Williams, L. M., Riley, L. A., Risch, G. S., & Dickel, C. T. (1999). *Ministry to interchurch marriages: A national study*. Omaha, Nebraska: Creighton University.
[39] This information is found in the couple's resource entitled, *When you intermarry: A Resource for inter-Christian, intercultural couples, par-*

ents and families. It is offered here to ensure that clergy and lay leaders review this important information.

[40] For more information regarding human development theory and social ecological theory please consult the following resource: Boss, P. G., Doherty, W. J., LaRossa, R., Schumm, W. R., & Steinmetz, S. K. (1993). *Sourcebook of family theories and methods: A contextual approach*. New York: Plenum Press.

[41] *Warning!* If you discover that the information contained in chapters 7 – 11 is ineffectual as you counsel spouses and couples, it is likely that there are other underlying issues that require additional attention and expertise. In these cases, it may be wise to refer such couples to a marriage therapist in whom you have some confidence. In collaboration with this professional, both you and he / she can continue working with this couple. You might consider working on their religious and spiritual needs while the couple's therapist might address the underlying individual, couple and family psychological and systemic issues.

[42] You should also quickly notice that this information will not contradict Orthodox theology and can easily be utilized as you seek to provide pastoral guidance and spiritual direction.

[43] The clergy and lay workers manual for intermarried couples and the intermarried couple's resource are intended to be utilized together. As such, the information pertaining to the challenges that dating couples encounter generally exists in the intermarried couple's resource.

[44] For more information consider the following resource: Wallerstein, J. S., Lewis, J. M. & Blakeslee, S. (2000). *The unexpected legacy of divorce: A 25 year landmark study*. New York: Hyperion.

[45] Waite, L. J., Browning, D., Doherty, W. J., Gallagher, M., Luo, Y., & Stanley, S. (2002). *Does divorce make people happy?* New York: NY: Institute for American Values.

[46] Being familiar with one or two professionals is important today in this litigious society. While clergy are generally protected from most lawsuits, total immunity from prosecution no longer exists. Recent test cases suggest that clergy and lay leaders are culpable when it is determined that they have exceeded their purview of expertise. Remembering your limitations, and referring when in doubt, is a wise

approach. Cultivating a collaborative relationship with one or two trusted professionals can prove to enhance God's work.

[47] For more information, consult the following reference: Koenig, H. G. (1998). *A handbook of religion and mental health.* San Diego: Academic Press.

[48] For more information, consult the following reference: Weaver, A. J., Koenig, H. G., & Larson, D. B. (1997). Marriage and family therapists and the clergy: A need for clinical collaboration, training, and research. *Journal of Marital and Family Therapy*. 23, 13-25.

[49] For more information, consider the following resource: Koenig, H.G. (1998). *Handbook of religion and mental health.* San Diego: Academic Press.

[50]The clergy and lay workers manual for intermarried couples and the intermarried couple's resource, *When you intermarry: A Resource for inter-Christian, intercultural couples, parents and families,* are intended to be utilized together. As such, much of the information pertaining to the challenges that engaged couples encounter generally exists in the intermarried couple's resource.

[51] As previously indicated, while clergy are generally protected from most lawsuits, total immunity from prosecution no longer exists. Recent test cases suggest that clergy and lay leaders are culpable when it is determined that they have exceeded their purview of expertise. Remembering your limitations, and referring when in doubt, is a wise approach. Cultivating a collaborative relationship with one or two trusted professionals can prove to enhance God's work.

[52] If you are unfamiliar with a trusted professional, the following web site may prove helpful in your efforts to begin identifying a competent professional: www.aamft.org. This site contains a therapist locator together with their profiles to help you begin acquainting yourself with psychotherapists in your area.

[53] To assist you, please be aware of your Hierarch's directives. The pastoral guidelines in Chapter 12 should also prove useful, together with the following resource: Vrame, A. (1997). *Intermarriage: Orthodox perspectives*. Brookline, MA: Holy Cross Orthodox Press.

[54] The following resource clearly reinforces this point: Stanley, S., Trathen, D., McCain, S & Bryan, M. (1998). *A lasting promise: A Christian guide to fighting for your marriage*. San Francisco: Jossey-Bass Publishers

[55] To assist you in this process, refer couples to the last two chapters of the intermarried couple's resource. These chapters will acquaint couples with the Orthodox Church's pastoral directives. This information will also help couples consider the pros and cons of entering an inter-Christian, intercultural marriage.
[56] Joanides, C., Joanning, H., & Keoughan. (2000). Towards an understanding of religious people's perception and lived experiences of religion and ethnicity: Implications for marriage and family therapists. *Journal of Family Social Work*. 4, p. 79-97.
[57] For more information about this, refer the couple to the following resource: Arp, D. H., Arp, C. S., Stanley, S. M., Markman, H. J. & Blumberg, S. L. (2000). *Fighting for your empty nest marriage*. San Francisco: Josey Bass.
[58] In this resource, the term intramarried is utilized to describe couples who are members of the same faith and cultural background.
[59] *Culture shock* refers to the emotional disruption that persons experience when they find themselves in a social setting that is unfamiliar with their own. In these cases, it is not unusual for such persons to experience a sense of strangeness for a considerable amount of time.
[60] For more information, consider Chapter 7 in the intermarried couple's resource. This chapter concerns itself directly with extended family challenges.
[61] Marriages are most vulnerable to ending in divorce during the first seven years. Research suggests that many marriages fail because couples are either unable or unprepared to negotiate the challenges they confront. For more information, consult the following resource: Gottman, J. (1999). *The Marriage clinic: A scientifically based marital therapy*. New York: Norton & Company.
[62] Joanides, C. (1996). Collaborative family therapy with religious family systems. *Journal of Family Psychotherapy*. 7, 19-35.
[63] Research indicates that pastors are among the first to be contacted when couples are encountering marital problems. For more information consider the following reference: Weaver, A. J., Koenig, H. G., & Larson, D. B. (1997). Marriage and family therapists and the clergy: A need for clinical collaboration, training, and research. *Journal of Marital and Family Therapy*. 23, 13-25.

[64] Results from the IRP suggest that intermarried couples' relationship with the Greek Orthodox priest is a crucial factor in their decision to worship in the Orthodox Church.
[65] I realize that this advice runs against the grain of what many priests have been taught, since we've been schooled within a tradition that favors a directive counseling approach. So, please keep in mind that we live in a litigious society and your skills working with couples are limited. Please also remember that outcome studies evaluating clinical modalities indicate that distressed people are more likely to experience long term positive effects from counseling when they take a proactive role in the therapeutic process. Less directive approaches tend to enhance a couple's efforts to develop conflict resolution skills. Of course, in cases where there is some form of abuse detected, directive approaches must be utilized.
[66] For a good description of domestic violence as it pertains to members of the Greek Orthodox Archdiocese of America, please consult the following reference: Geanacopoulos, Paulette. (2000, Fall). *Domestic violence: A training manual for the Greek Orthodox Community.* (Available from the Greek Orthodox Ladies Philoptochos Society, 345 East 74 Street, New York, NY 10021).
[67] To help you locate such an individual, consider logging onto the American Association of Marital and Family Therapy's Web site: www.AAMFT.org. This site has a therapist locator that you can utilize to find a licensed professional in your area.
[68] For more information see the following resource: Doherty, William (2001). *Take back your marriage*. New York: Guilford Press.
[69] When social scientists utilize this concept, they are referring to young adults' efforts to separate themselves from their parents in an effort to form their own opinions about the world around them.
[70] For more information, consider the following resource: Koenig, H. G. (1998). *Handbook of religion and mental health*. San Diego: Academic Press.
[71] For more information about these four categories please refer to the following reference: Crohn, J. (1995). *Mixed matches: How to create successful interracial, interethnic, and interfaith relationships*, New York: Fawcett Columbine.
[72] For more information about this stage of the marital life cycle consult the following reference: Arp, D. H., Arp, C. S., Stanley, S. M.,

Markman, H. J. & Blumberg. S. (2000). *Fighting for your empty nest marriage*. San Francisco: Jossey-Bass.
[73] Many of these couples can profit from the information contained in the intermarried couples' resource entitled, *When you intermarry: A Resource for inter-Christian, intercultural couples, parents and families.*
[74] I recommend the intermarried couple's resource. Reading about the challenges that intermarried couples face could enhance conflicted intermarried couple's efforts to find some mutually agreeable resolutions.
[75] These figures are based on research studies that have examined marital and family therapists' work with couples and families.
[76] Please refer to Chapter 12 for further information regarding the Orthodox Church's pastoral guidelines. Additionally, should a pastoral challenge emerge that requires more feedback, always consult your Hierarch for clarification before providing the couple with information. It is better for you to claim ignorance than to provide misinformation that will only further exacerbate the situation.
[77] We live in a society that values the scientific approach. By grounding your remarks on research, you will be lending credibility to your observations.
[78] I am deeply grateful to Dr. Lewis Patsavos for his many valued contributions to this chapter. His expertise and astute observations made a decided positive difference.
[79] For additional information, consider the following resources: Constantelos, D. J. (1997). Mixed marriages in historical perspective. In A. C. Vrame (Ed.), *Interfaith marriage: Orthodox perspectives*. Brookline, MA: Holy Cross Orthodox Press. Constantelos, D. J. (1999). Church and family in the Greek Orthodox society from the Byzantine era to the present-day United States: Problems and issues. In S. J. Tremberis, H. J. Psomiades & A. Karpathakis (Eds.), *Greek American families: Traditions and transformations*. New York, NY: Pella Publishing Company. Patsavos, L. (1997). A canonical response to intra-Christian and inter-Christian marriage. In A. C. Vrame (Ed.) *InterMarriage: Orthodox perspectives.* Brookline, MA: Holy Cross Orthodox Press. Patsovos, L. & Joanides, C. (2000). Interchurch marriages: An Orthodox perspective. *International academy for marital spirituality review*. 6, 215-223.
[80] This theological concept refers to a timely deviation the Church might take from a canonically established rule. Such a decision might

be made to preserve the unity of the Church and facilitate its faithfuls' religious and spiritual development.

[81]Unlike the Roman Catholic Church, which has a centralized form of government, the Orthodox Church is a family of self-governing Churches referred to as autocephalous Churches.

[82] See Demetrios J. Constantelos, (1997). Mixed marriage in historical perspective. In (A. C. Vrame, Ed.). *Intermarriage: Orthodox perspectives*. Brookline, MA: Holy Cross Orthodox Press.

[83] According to the Special Regulations and Uniform Parish Regulations of the GOA (Article VI, Section 1), "Any person, eighteen years of age or over, who has been baptized according to the rites of the Church, or was received into the Church through chrismation, who lives according to the faith and canons of the Church, who has met his financial obligation to the Parish and abides by the regulations herein and the by-laws of the Parish, is a member in good standing of the Parish."

[84] The term sponsor is a generic term that refers to either the *paranymphos* or *paranymphy* who exchanges the rings and crowns during the Sacrament of Marriage or the godparent during the Sacrament of Baptism.

[85] Research indicates that the attrition rate among this population is substantial among other faith groups. In some cases, studies show a 50% rate of loss. For more information see, Lawler, M. G., Markey, B., Williams, L. M., Riley, L. A., Risch, G. S., & Dickel, C. T. (1999). *Ministry to interchurch marriages: A national study*. Omaha, Nebraska: Creighton University. Lehrer, E. (1998). Religious intermarriage in the United States: Determinants and trends. *Social Science Research*, 27, 245-263.

[86] In our efforts to find this balance, it is important to remember that as early as the fourth and fifth centuries BC, the Greek orator Isacrates emphasized the universal character of Hellenism in *Panegyrikos (Encomium of Athens)*: He states, "The name 'Hellenes' suggests no longer a race, but a way of thinking, and... the title 'Hellenes' is applied rather to those who share our culture than those who share our blood."

[87] Pehanich, E. (2000). What actually works to keep kids involved in the church. *Orthodox Christian education commission news*. 20, 1-2.

[88] The following resource should prove extremely help: Rouvelas, M. (1993). *A guide to Greek traditions and customs in America*. 2nd edition. Bethesda, MD: Nea Attiki Press.
[89] For more information about Marriage Savers write to Michael McManus, 9311 Harrington Drive, Potomac, MD or visit the following Web site: www.marriagesavers.org.
[90] Father Charles Joanides is presently conducting Marriage Building Workshops. For more information about these workshops, contact Father Charles.
[91] For more information consider the following references: Larson, J. H. (January, 1999). Comprehensive premarital assessment questionnaires: Bringing science to premarital counseling. *Family Therapy News*. pp. 15, 17.
[92] A resource for intermarried couples is now available entitled: *When you intermarry: A resource for inter-Christian, intercultural couples, parents and families*. It has been developed to be used when you conduct premarital counseling with engaged couples from different religious and cultural backgrounds.
[93] If you choose to discuss this information with either one couple or in a group setting with multiple couples, the questionnaire at end of this chapter should facilitate your work.
[94] Harley, W. F., (2001). *Fall in love stay in love*. Grand Rapids, MI: Fleming H. Revell.